Every Bush Is Burning

A Practical Theology for Biblical Integration

Kelly Hayes

Every Bush Is Burning: A Practical Theology for Biblical Integration

This work was developed as a part of Kelly Hayes's doctoral project at The Southern Baptist Theological Seminary.

The Southern Baptist Theological Seminary has permission to reproduce and disseminate that document in any form by any means for purposes chosen by the Seminary, including, without limitation, preservation or instruction.

Scripture quotations are taken from THE HOLY BIBLE, NEW INTERNATIONAL VERSION®, NIV® Copyright © 1973, 1978, 1984, 2011 by Biblica, Inc.® Used by permission. All rights reserved worldwide.

Cover art by Jessica M. Hayes.

With thanks to the staff and faculty at The King's Academy, especially Barb Osterrieder, David Wolff, and Sandy Hill.

Contents

Introduction: A Note from the Author..................................1

PART ONE

THE BIBLICAL AND THEOLOGICAL BASIS FOR
BIBLICAL INTEGRATION 5

Chapter 1

The Teacher's Pastoral Role 7

Chapter 2

The Teacher's Prophetic Role 13

Chapter 3

The Teacher's Priestly Role................................27

Chapter 4

The Teacher's Kingly Role 39

PART TWO

THE THEORETICAL, PRACTICAL, AND HISTORICAL
BASIS FOR BIBLICAL INTEGRATION 49

Chapter Five

What Makes Education Distinctly Christian? 51

Chapter 6

Understanding Biblical Integration...................65

PART THREE

Curriculum Articles 77
01: Starting with Honesty
02: A Vision of Success

Training 1

The Incarnational Teacher 83
03: Understanding Incarnation
04: Reenacting the Gospel

Training 2

The Intentional Teacher 90
05: The Bible and Biblical Integration
06: How to Handle Our Weapon – What Not to Do
07: How to Handle Our Weapon – What to Do
08: Integration Helps the Teacher and Student
09: Purposeful Course Design
10: It's Not an Add-On When It's in the DNA
11: Assessment and Biblical Integration

Training 3

The Instigating Teacher 113
12: Healthy Conflict and the Teacher as Trainer
13: Essential Conflict Questions
14: Designing Conflict Questions and Strategies
15: You Are the System

About the Author 126

Introduction: A Note from the Author

Dear Christian Educator,

You are a preacher. It might seem odd to think about yourself in that way and you might contend, "No, I don't preach. I teach." But, in your teaching, you have the duty and opportunity to share and show God's truth every day. Your classroom is a sanctuary and your lesson plans are liturgy. Yes, you are a preacher. Martin Lloyd-Jones explains, "What is preaching? Logic on fire! Eloquent reason!... What is the chief end of preaching? ... to give men and women a sense of God and His presence."[1] It is this task that Christian teachers are called to engage in — we are giving our students a robust understanding of God and his presence through teaching. My goal in this book is to equip you to understand and successfully engage in the mission to which God has called you.

This will not be easy work. Biblically integrated teaching can be challenging. However, it is necessary and it is significant. T. S. Eliot said, "When the Christian faith is not only felt, but thought, it has practical results which may be inconvenient."[2]

It is nothing new for the preaching of God's message to be difficult. Even the prophet Jeremiah, for example, struggled as he faithfully shared God's Word.[3] But, difficult things are often the most worthwhile. Though communicating God's

---

[1] D. Martyn Lloyd-Jones, *Preaching and Preachers* (Grand Rapids: Zondervan, 2012), 110. Kindle.

[2] T. S. Eliot, *Christianity and Culture* (1940; repr., Eliot Press, 2013), 6. Kindle.

[3] F. L. Cross and Elizabeth A. Livingstone, eds., *The Oxford Dictionary of the Christian Church* (Oxford; New York: Oxford University Press, 2005), 871.

message was demanding, Jeremiah could not help but share. If he closed his mouth, it was as if there were flames shut up in his bones or fire within his heart (Jer 20:9). He had to let it out. Though costly, preaching is natural for those who know and love God. It was natural for Jeremiah and, likewise, it is natural for us.

The Christian message has always been foolishness to those who don't believe, but it is also the very power of God to those who are being saved (1 Cor 1:18). God, in his immense wisdom and power (1 Cor 1:25), has designed a world that is custom-made to display his glory (Ps 8:1). C.S. Lewis artfully explained, "Every bush (could we but perceive it) is a Burning Bush."[4] There is not a subject that we could teach that is disconnected from God and his glory. The Christian worldview begs to be explored and applied in science, math, and history. And God has chosen you to preach through the megaphone of the classroom.

God has given us everything we need—hearts on fire and a world of burning bushes so that we can share logic aflame by preaching Him. Every course, syllabus, lesson, assessment, and class-period is a chance to make much of who He is and help students orient their lives in response. As students learn his world, we want them to learn Him. We are desperate for them to know the Artist through his art. The cover of this book is intended as a useful visual representation of our goal: to bring out the color and fire in an otherwise black-and-white world. Christian educators must highlight God and his ways as we teach the subjects that He invented.

The content of this book is designed to help you do just that. Part 1 contains a biblical and theological rationale for living out your pastoral role as a teacher. Part 2 thoughtfully examines the core theoretical and practical elements of biblical integration in the classroom. Part 3 contains a sequence of short, practical articles and activities which are designed to be

---

[4]C. S. Lewis, *Letters to Malcolm: Chiefly on Prayer* (Orlando: Harcourt, 1963), 75.

used in conjunction with the *Every Bush is Burning* biblical integration training. However, these materials could also easily be employed for personal growth or small-group discussion.

Parts 1 and 2 are written with more academic and philosophical sensibilities while Part 3 is written in a popular style. Readers may be unfamiliar with some of the terminology used in the first two sections, but this is to be expected. Do not be discouraged or frustrated if there are some elements that you do not grasp right away. Reading this book is meant to stretch and challenge. Various helps (summaries, questions, "nerd notes," and practical points) have been included along the way to serve you as you think and grow.

My prayer is that this book will be a servant to you as you strive to serve Christ and your students.

KELLY HAYES

JUNE 17, 2017

PART ONE

THE BIBLICAL AND THEOLOGICAL BASIS FOR BIBLICAL INTEGRATION

Education is an essential task of the Christian community, but what kind of education is pleasing to the Lord? Teachers are to build others up by explaining God's gracious initiative in reaching out to mankind, and urging a response of loving obedience.[5] Jesus Himself is the perfect example of an effective teacher.[6] In Part 1, the case is made that effective teachers follow Christ's example and leadership.

While Jesus was called "master" or "rabbi" by Matthew, Mark, and John, the word *epistates* was used by Luke. *Epistates* means "schoolmaster," which would have been a term more familiar outside of the Jewish community.[7] The Great Commission concludes with the Schoolmaster's command to make disciples by "teaching them to obey everything I have commanded you" (Matt 28:20). John F. Blanchard expounds on this passage explaining, "The ministry of the Christian school must begin with the saving gospel of our Lord Jesus Christ but it dare not stop there."[8] How should the Christian educator proceed with and from the gospel? Following the example of Christ, teachers must show God as the answer to life's fundamental worldview questions (Prov 1:7), highlight the preeminence and power of

---

[5]David L. Turner, "Teach, Teacher," in *Evangelical Dictionary of Biblical Theology*, ed. Walter A. Elwell, Baker Reference Library (Grand Rapids: Baker, 1996), 757.

[6]Jan H. Nylund, "Teacher," in *The Lexham Bible Dictionary*, ed. John D. Barry et al., Logos electronic ed. (Bellingham, WA: Lexham, 2016), n.p.

[7]Robert Stagg, "Rabbi," in *Holman Illustrated Bible Dictionary*, ed. Chad Brand et al. (Nashville: Holman Bible, 2003), 1360.

[8]John F. Blanchard, Jr., "The Christian School," in *Baker's Dictionary of Practical Theology*, ed. Ralph G. Turnbull (Grand Rapids: Baker, 1967), 443.

Christ as He holds all things together (Col 1:15-17), and amplify God's two messengers: his world and his Word (Ps 19).

Chapter 1

The Teacher's Pastoral Role

SIMPLE SUMMARY

CHRISTIAN EDUCATORS ARE PASTORS WHO WORK IN THE SCHOOL SETTING. OUR GOAL, AS TEACHERS, IS TO SHEPHERD STUDENTS TOWARD SUCCESS THROUGH AN UNDERSTANDING OF LIFE THAT LEADS TO GODLINESS. JESUS, THE GOOD SHEPHERD, IS THE ULTIMATE EXAMPLE AND GUIDE FOR TEACHERS. THIS CHAPTER LOOKS TO CHRIST IN ORDER TO DISCERN WHAT BEING A PASTORAL TEACHER IS ALL ABOUT.

Education is an intentional attempt to control, direct, or manage learning to attain a specific outcome.[9] Teachers spend a great deal of time designing broad curricula and individual lesson plans that aim at desired outcomes. They want students to know how to read, solve, know, and communicate effectively. However, the Christian educator must keep the most important outcome in mind always. Which need are teachers most dedicated to meeting?

The need is not rooted in knowledge or skill alone. The deepest and most lasting need for all people is right relationship with Christ. The apostle John said that this relationship with God is the definition of eternal life (John 17:3). Therefore, as George Knight writes, Christian educators, regardless of subject, should strive "to educate people in the light of their greatest need—Jesus."[10] Some may object by saying that this portrays Christian teachers as if they were

---

[9]George R. Knight, *Philosophy & Education: An Introduction in Christian Perspective*, 4th ed. (Berrien Springs, MI: Andrews University Press, 2006), 10.

[10]Ibid., 281.

pastors. However, in a very real sense, Christian school teachers are pastors. Knight explains,

> The major difference between the roles of pastors and teachers in our day has to do with the current division of labor. In twenty-first-century society, the Christian teacher may be seen as one who pastors in a "school" context, while the pastor is one who teaches in the "larger religious community." It should and must consciously be realized that their function is essentially the same, even though by today's definitions they are in charge of different divisions of the Lord's vineyard.[11]

The word "pastor" means "shepherd," and refers to the activity of shepherding souls.[12] The duty of the pastor is to build up Christ's body and counter false teaching.[13] All Christian educators must be involved in these practices daily. Their flocks may sit at desks rather than in pews, but teachers are shepherds nonetheless.

Since the identity of the teacher is pastoral, the practice of teaching must take on pastoral aims. To deny the Christian leadership of the teacher is to forfeit what makes Christian education Christian. For example, the Christian biology teacher is a Christian teacher before a science teacher. In that vein, the teacher knows that all lesson content is also spiritual. All things are from, through, and for Christ (Rom 11:36). All math equations, literary themes, and historical events declare his glory and must be taught accordingly. The goal of this

---

[11] Ibid., 211.

[12] F. L. Cross and Elizabeth A. Livingstone, eds., *The Oxford Dictionary of the Christian Church*, (Oxford: Oxford University Press, 2005), 1237.

[13] Walter A. Elwell and Barry J. Beitzel, "Pastor," in *Baker Encyclopedia of the Bible* (Grand Rapids: Baker, 1988), 1618.

chapter is to begin to provide a biblical, theological, and philosophical foundation for the role of the educator as pastor through the practice of biblical integration.

The Master Teacher

To live into their role as pastoral educators, Christian school teachers should look to the ultimate practical theologian, integrator, and educator — the Messiah. Christ is the ultimate teacher and He identified Himself as the Way, the Truth, and the Life (John 14:6). Each of these elements are essential parts of education. Students seek the way — they want to know what is best, and right, and good. They seek truth — they want to know what is actual and real. They also desire life — each wants to find meaning, purpose, and value. How can true education exist without being built from and toward Christ-centered theology? It cannot. People can search, but the only way to answer is to turn to the Lord. Paul explains that God has orchestrated all of life "so that they would seek him and perhaps reach out for him and find him, though he is not far from any one of us" (Acts 17:27).

The integrating teacher points to the Way, Truth, and Life in every

> **Quick Question**
> Do you see your daily work as pointing students toward the way, truth, and life? Why or why not?

way possible. This kind of instructor is devoted to teaching all things in a way that shows the characteristics and character of God. The habit for too long has been to teach truth apart from the Truth, which has led to a rationalism that, for instance, is more committed to the idea that man cannot rise from the dead than to the idea that God can do anything He pleases. The foundational presupposition of rationalism cannot do what the presupposition of the Christian God can: offer a credible and miraculous Christ.[14]

Therefore, the task of biblical integration, or building from and toward God in all things, is the necessary task of the Christian educator. "The Son is the radiance of God's glory and the exact representation of his being, sustaining all things by his powerful word" (Heb 1:3). Learners must learn Christ who sustains all. Also, they must learn Him in full connection to and context of his world. It follows, then, that instructors of any things must teach the One who sustains all things in everything. Biblical integration is the task the teacher takes up to help the student here. This integration advances learning beyond Sunday school or the simple accumulation of knowledge.

Jesus declared that his role on earth was as a teacher when He said, "The reason I was born and came into the world is to testify to the truth" (John 18:37). Christian educators carry this same goal — testifying to the Truth by teaching truths. Teachers should examine the Master Teacher and learn from his message, means, and methods. The Bible describes three ways in which the Son of Man came: "the Son of Man came not to be served but to serve, and to give his life as a ransom for many" (Mark 10: 45); "the Son of Man came to seek and to save the lost" (Luke 19: 10); and "the Son of Man has come eating and drinking" (Luke 7: 34).[15] The Servant offered Good News through the means of relationships. In Him, rational, behavioral, and relational truths were united with eternal effect.

---

[14]Francis Schaeffer, *The Francis A. Schaeffer Trilogy: Three Essential Books in One Volume* (Wheaton, IL: Crossway, 1990), 53.

[15]Tim Chester, *A Meal with Jesus: Discovering Grace, Community, and Mission around the Table* (Wheaton, IL: Crossway, 2011), 12.

Jesus' three roles of Way, Truth, and Life are often communicated in another way. He led the way as King, told the truth as Prophet, and shepherded people toward life as Priest.[16] He was no mere theological technician who had settled for communicating concepts of truth. He was a passionate and caring teacher—a good teacher (Mark 10:17). He was invested in a ministry of synergism that united rational, behavioral, and relational elements.[17] He was an axiological, epistemological, and metaphysical instructor. The teacher who brings these elements together follows the example of Christ as teacher. As a follower of Christ, the Christian educator must serve as prophet, priest, and king to the class, teaching others to think, value, and do what pleases the Father. William Yount explains, "It should be no surprise, then,

> **Nerd Note**
> *Axiology* has to do with value—what something is worth.
> *Epistemology* is related to understanding truth.
> *Metaphysics* deals with the big/deep questions of the universe.

that the Master Teacher reflected the Triad in His own teaching ministry. God created us in His Image—thinker, feeler, doer—and Jesus reflected that triadic perspective in His life and work as Prophet, Priest, and King."[18]

Theologian John Frame is known for a similar tri-perspectival approach to theology.[19] He recommends looking at knowledge from normative, situational, and existential perspectives. These perspectives can align with epistemology,

---

[16]Yount offers a short but helpful summary of the teacher's role as prophet, priest, and king in his book. William Yount, "The Teacher as Minister," in *Called to Teach: An Introduction to the Ministry of Teaching* (Nashville: B & H, 1999), 223-31.

[17]Ibid., 15.

[18]William Yount, *Created to Learn: A Christian Teacher's Introduction to Educational Psychology*, 2nd ed. (Nashville: B & H, 2010), locs. 9221-23, Kindle.

[19]John Frame, "A Primer on Perspectivalism (Revised 2008)," June 6, 2012, accessed December 31, 2016, http://frame-poythress.org/a-primer-on-perspectivalism-revised-2008/.

metaphysics, and axiology. Both Yount and Frame provide corresponding frameworks that include three significant questions of philosophy — what is real? what is truth? what is valuable?[20]

Christ is real. Christ is truth. Christ is ultimately valuable. The following section provides a scriptural basis for biblical integration by expounding on how teachers can embrace their roles as prophets, priests, and kings. In representing Jesus to students in these ways, teachers embrace their pastoral role and faithfully follow Christ.

Practical Point

The more like Jesus we are, the more effective and faithful we will be. The next three chapters will zoom in on what it looks like to take on each of the pastoral roles of prophet, priest, and king in the school setting.

---

[20]Yount, *Created to Learn*, locs. 1078-83.

Chapter 2

The Teacher's Prophetic Role

SIMPLE SUMMARY
WISE TEACHING IS GOD-CENTERED TEACHING. WE HAVE THE
OPPORTUNITY TO SHOW THAT EVERY AREA OF LIFE IS FROM AND
FOR THE LORD. HE IS THE ANSWER TO ALL OF LIFE'S BIG QUESTIONS.
THIS CHAPTER FOCUSES ON PROVERBS 1:7 AND HIGHLIGHTS THE
ROLE OF THE PROPHETIC TEACHER AS A TEACHER OF RIGHT
WORLDVIEW.

A prophet is one who speaks for God. God can speak to
a prophet in any way He deems suitable, but regardless of the
means through which God speaks, He wants "his prophets to
receive his message and the people to remember what he [has]
said."[21] Prophets are the Lord's mouthpiece. Since Christians
have God's message in the Bible, Christian teachers are called
to share those truths. God has spoken. No special gift beyond
the Bible and the Holy Spirit is required for speaking truth
confidently. As Easton explains, the Old Testament even tells
of "schools of prophets" where students could choose to go
and learn "to preach pure morality and the heart-felt worship
of Jehovah, and to act along and co-ordinately with the
priesthood and monarchy in guiding the state aright and
checking all attempts at illegality and tyranny."[22] The role of
prophet was complementary to kings and priests, but it was
one that a believer could choose to take up. The New

---

[21]Walter C. Kaiser, Jr., "Prophet, Prophetess, Prophecy," in *Evangelical Dictionary of Biblical Theology*, 644-45.

[22]M. G. Easton, *Easton's Bible Dictionary*, Logos electronic ed. (New York: Harper & Brothers, 1893), n.p.

₁estament explains that a prophet has the responsibility to edify and encourage believers.[23] It could be accurately said that a prophet is one who shares the Way, Truth, and Life. This sharing is a necessary role of all Christian educators.

One of the great tools that one must employ in the pastoral role of prophet, that all Christian teachers hold, is a right worldview. Jeff Myers and David A. Noebel state that a worldview is "a pattern of ideas, beliefs, convictions, and habits that help us make sense of God, the world, and our relationship to God and the world."[24] A worldview built upon a proper orientation toward and understanding of God as the foundation and goal of reality will affect the practice of teaching. It allows the prophet to speak for God through science, English, physical education, and all other course content. Worldview is the reason for specifically Christian schools.

> **Quick Question**
> What does it communicate to students if we teach a subject without showing how the material is connected to God?

Christian schools are established, Knight explains, because Christians hold to "a different set of philosophic foundations and educational boundaries from those of the larger culture."[25] A different set of foundations necessitates different educational constructs. Worldview commitments affect teaching because they set the foundation and aim of knowledge and learning. In other words, the school that embraces the Christian worldview allows teachers to function as prophets.

---

[23]Aaron C. Fenlason, "Prophets," in *Lexham Theological Wordbook*, Lexham Bible Reference Series, ed. Douglas Mangum et al., Logos electronic ed. (Bellingham, WA: Lexham, 2014), n.p.

[24]Jeff Myers and David A. Noebel, *Understanding the Times* (Manitou Springs, CO: Summit Ministries, 2015), 6.

[25]Knight, *Philosophy & Education*, 35.

From Prime Reality to Life-Orienting Commitments

The concept of worldview is intimately related to the goal of developing a redemptive theology of teaching. A worldview is a commitment[26] and the Christian worldview is a commitment to seeing reality as the God of the Bible presents it. James Sire offers eight basic questions that provide the foundation of a Christian worldview:

1. What is prime reality—the really real?
2. What is the nature of external reality, that is, the world around us?
3. What is a human being?
4. What happens to a person at death?
5. Why is it possible to know anything at all?
6. How do we know what is right and wrong?
7. What is the meaning of human history?
8. What personal, life-orienting core commitments are consistent with this worldview? [27]

According to Sire, a worldview is a "spiritual orientation more than it is a matter of the mind alone."[28] Before focusing on seeing the world correctly, one must open his eyes to the foundational reality of the Person of God. Right orientation toward God is the prerequisite for gaining understanding. Psalm 111:10 says, "The fear of the LORD is the beginning of wisdom; all who follow his precepts have good understanding. To him belongs eternal praise." God's Word is clear that wisdom starts and ends with Him. One who fears Him is on the path of wisdom. One who does not cannot grasp reality. Proverbs 9:10 clarifies, "The fear of the LORD is the beginning of wisdom, and knowledge of the Holy One is understanding." Understanding is directly equated to fearing

---

[26]James Sire, *The Universe Next Door: A Basic Worldview Catalog* (Westmont, IL: IVP, 2009), 20.

[27]Sire, *The Universe Next Door*, 22-23.

[28]Ibid., 20.

and revering God. Roger White clarifies the definition of the "fear of the Lord":

> The book of Proverbs affirms the fear of the Lord as the beginning of knowledge and wisdom. Here the fear of the Lord means a healthy reverence for God, not servile terror. It moves individuals from being exclusively self-referenced in their understanding to increasingly seeing all things and especially one's life journey oriented in and around God. . . This is a whole-hearted, whole-being response. Having such a deferential posture toward God and an accompanying intellectual modesty are core elements in the pilgrimage of life and learning.[29]

Proverbs 1:7 shares this idea in a particularly helpful way: "The fear of the LORD is the beginning of knowledge, but fools despise wisdom and instruction." The contrast here between knowledge and foolishness provides a good starting point for examining God as the foundation of everything. This passage provides a framework for examining the theme of wisdom and knowledge as found throughout Scripture. The following is a biblical survey launched from and toward the content of Proverbs 1:7. It seeks to engage with James Sire's eight worldview questions from a broadly biblical perspective with the foundational theme of Proverbs 1:7 — the fear of the Lord is the beginning of knowledge.

---

[29]Roger White, "Orienting to Truth North," in *Mapping Out Curriculum in Your Church: Cartography for Christian Pilgrims*, ed. James Estep, Roger White, and Karen Estep (Nashville: B & H, 2012), locs. 560-66, Kindle.

Proverbs 1:7 and Sire's Worldview Questions

The first seven verses in the book of Proverbs should naturally catch the eye of the teacher. The opening lines declare the intent—learning wisdom that leads to success in life.[30] While many may claim to hold the keys to wisdom, the Proverbs are not untested ideas from an unreliable source. This wisdom is connected to Solomon. The key concepts of Israel's wisest king (1 Kgs 3:12) are available to the reader, whether immature or wise, to come and grow. The only group excluded from learning is the fool who will not listen.[31]

The author claims that the understanding and application of Proverbs' content will lead to flourishing. This is a guidebook that leads to wisdom, discipline, success, righteousness, justice, equity, knowledge, and discernment. This biblical content is applied to all of life. Duane Garrett explains, "By this book, one can learn the principles that determine success or failure in the major arenas of human activity, including business, personal relationships, family life, and community life."[32] Christian educators daily invest in preparing students to be successful in these areas and would be wise to listen. As Solomon says, only a fool would reject what Scripture offers here.

God Is the Foundation

Proverbs 1:7 contains the final line of Solomon's introductory statements, but shares the starting point for knowledge—fear of the Lord. If one does not treat God rightly, it does not matter how well he handles any other area of life.

---

[30]Duane A. Garrett, *Proverbs, Ecclesiastes, Song of Songs*, The New American Commentary, vol. 14 (Nashville: Broadman & Holman, 1993), 67.

[31]Tremper Longman III, *Proverbs*, in vol. 5 of *Zondervan Illustrated Bible Backgrounds Commentary*, ed. John H. Walton (Grand Rapids: Zondervan, 2009), 471.

[32]Garrett, *Proverbs, Ecclesiastes, Song of Songs*, 67.

Without a right view of God, there is no opportunity for true flourishing in any area. God is the blessing that functions as the foundation of all other blessings.[33] To answer Sire's first question, He is the prime reality.

This verse offers a logical argument for how to live life well. Essentially, wisdom leads to successful living and successful living is rightly revering the Lord.[34] For example, success in business is handling work in ways that honor God. Success in relationships is loving God by loving others. Godliness is a key in understanding wisdom — every success is built upon success in relationship with God. For what benefit is there in gaining the world but losing one's soul? (Mark 8:36).

> **Quick Question**
> How do you generally envision success? How do you think your students see it?

Teachers who give the students everything other than Christ are, in sum, giving them nothing. In Colossians 1:28, Paul said of Christ, "He is the one we proclaim, admonishing and teaching everyone with all wisdom, so that we may present everyone fully mature in Christ." How does one warn and teach with all wisdom? This is only accomplished by proclaiming Christ. How does one present others as mature in Christ? This is only done by proclaiming Him. God is the starting point of wisdom and knowledge. Educators must start at the beginning by acknowledging God as the foundation and inviting students to choose to do the same.

To emphasize God as the foundation of all knowledge is not to say that all who do not honor God know nothing. It is to say that they do not see the "big picture."[35] Tremper Longman uses the example of sailing. One may know how to

---

[33]Richard J. Clifford, *Proverbs: A Commentary*, The Old Testament Library (Louisville: Westminster John Knox, 1999), 34.

[34]Ibid.

[35]Tremper Longman III, *Proverbs*, Baker Commentary on the Old Testament (Grand Rapids: Baker, 2006), 101.

sail, but not know the One who made the winds and seas. If he did, he might respond differently.[36] Note how the disciples responded when they understood Jesus' identity as Lord of wind and wave. They truly began to fear Him as God. Being terrified, they asked one another, "Who is this? Even the wind and the waves obey him!" (Matt 8:27). Reverence was a needed part of their discipleship process. They grasped Christ as prime reality and saw that the world He had made was an arena for his glory. They began to see Him as the power beneath the water and atmosphere. They had previously mastered sailing, but they were ignorant as to Christ being the power behind the mighty winds that moved their fishing vessels.

God Is the Source

Not only is God the foundation of wisdom, He is also the source of wise living. Proverbs 1:1-7 is clear that wisdom puts the individual in a position to succeed in life and godliness.[37] However, this wisdom is only present and active through the power of God. Second Peter 1:2-3 says that grace and peace are abundantly available through the knowledge of God and that it is his power that gives everything needed for a godly life. There is a clear connection here between knowledge and wise living. There is no wisdom from God without knowing Him. Bruce Waltke writes, "Wisdom is inseparable from knowledge."[38] Godly life is only possible "through knowledge of Him who called us by his own glory and goodness" (2 Pet 1:3). In other words, the beginning of knowledge is knowledge of God.

---

[36]Longman, *Proverbs*, 101.

[37]Clifford, *Proverbs*, 36.

[38]Bruce K. Waltke, *The Book of Proverbs*, The New International Commentary on the Old Testament (Grand Rapids: Eerdmans, 2004), 77.

True knowledge of God will shape the way a person thinks and lives. When grasped, fear of the Lord is more than mental assent. Knowledge becomes wisdom when it is enacted. Proverbs speaks of folly as the opposite of wisdom. Folly is more than just ignorance, but ungodly action.[39] Waltke explains, "A person could memorize the book of Proverbs and still lack wisdom if it did not affect his heart, which informs behavior."[40] Fear of God is important—it is knowledge that alters behavior. One who knows the power of a speeding car does not walk into the street without looking first. There is respect for the weight of a moving vehicle. Similarly, one who knows the power of the mighty God does not live without considering the weight of his will and ways. Tremper Longman III expounds,

> Only fools would not be afraid of a being who has the power of life and death over them. Such persons do not understand their place in the cosmos and thus do not know how to act in the world. All other wisdom builds on this point, and there is no wisdom without it.[41]

In acknowledging that humans must know their place, Longman speaks to Sire's third question—"What is a human being?"[42] Wisdom tells the created to live well in light of the Creator. In Matthew 10:28, Jesus stated this idea by saying, "Do not be afraid of those who kill the body but cannot kill the soul. Rather, be afraid of the One who can destroy both soul and body in hell." Fearing the Lord must be informed by the recognition of his power to destroy, but there is another side to revering Him. Believers should be in awe of Him

[39]Clifford, *Proverbs*, 35.

[40]Waltke, *The Book of Proverbs*, 77.

[41]Longman, *Proverbs*, 104.

[42]Sire, *The Universe Next Door*, 22.

because He is also "able to do immeasurably more than all we ask or imagine, according to his power that is at work within us" (Eph 3:20). Wisdom recognizes what He can do for and in people as well. A person created in God's image (Gen 1:27) can be conformed to it as well (Rom 8:29).

God is an unlimited source for limited man, so it is appropriate to ask with Sire, "What happens to a person at death?"[43] Mark 10 includes the story of a man who had lived a morally exemplary life by society's standards. However, apart from God, there was no eternal life for him (Mark 10:27). He was unwise because he was unwilling to give up his earthly wealth to gain eternal riches (Mark 10:22). The beginning of knowledge is to understand that there is no life or godliness without God on this earth or beyond it. In Philippians 2:13, Paul explained, "It is God who works in you to will and to act in order to fulfill his good purpose." Sanctification and salvation are both accomplished by his strength. He is the power source for wise living and mankind is eternally reliant on Him for that power.

God Is the Substance

Sire's fifth question is, "Why is it possible to know anything at all?"[44] Simply put, humans can know God because He has made Himself known (Rom 10:20). Hebrews 1:1-2 says, "In the past God spoke to our ancestors through the prophets at many times and in various ways, but in these last days he has spoken to us by his Son, whom he appointed heir of all things, and through whom also he made the universe." He is a God who desires to know people and to be known by them (Gal 4:9).

God's relational identity is innately connected to the goal of the Christian educator. Teachers aim to practice their

---

[43]Sire, *The Universe Next Door*, 22.

[44]Ibid.

pastoral role by pointing students to the God who wants to be known. It is only in God, who is the source of power, that students can find success in life and godliness. Teachers want students to thrive through knowing God and living into God's good, perfect, and pleasing will (Rom 12:2). Jesus said that his people are like branches and He is like the vine (John 15:5). Nothing is possible apart from Him, which includes all knowledge. Knowing Him is a prerequisite to knowing anything else fully. Christian teachers must recognize this in all their teaching.

Sire's sixth question seeks to identify moral foundations — how does one know what is right and wrong? This question is an extension of his fifth question and the answer is related as well. Knowing what is right is tied up in knowing the God who is right. Jesus explained morality in these terms by summing up the Law in two commands: love God with everything and love others as self (Matt 22:36-40). Ethics are defined in terms of relationship. Those who love God do right.

Roland E. Murphy states that the intention of the book of Proverbs is clearly communicated: "To pass on traditional wisdom with a strong religious orientation. . . . The message can be summarized: Wisdom brings life."[45] However, his assessment of the book's intention, while true, may not be deep enough. Wisdom does bring life, but that life is in God alone. Wisdom is only accessible through Him. Christ holds the words of life, so where else can one turn? (John 6:68). Or again, what does a man gain if he owns the world but loses his soul? (Mark 8:36).

Paul calls believers to set their minds on things above because Christ is life (Col 3:1, 4). There is no life apart from Him. He is the foundation and He is the source, but He is also the substance. Perhaps rather than saying only wisdom brings

[45]Roland E. Murphy, *Wisdom Literature: Job, Proverbs, Ruth, Canticles, Ecclesiastes, and Esther*, The Forms of Old Testament Literature 13 (Grand Rapids: Eerdmans, 1981), 53.

life, one might say that wisdom is only in God who is life. Moral choices are a function of a relationship with God, are possible because of God, and aim toward Him and his glory.

God Is the Goal

God is more than a means to an end — He is the end. He is the aim and reward of believers. Those who fear and love Him see Him as their ultimate desire. There can be no perfection or satisfaction without Him. Those who would be satisfied in eternal paradise apart from his presence have not been converted by the gospel.[46] This idea is clearly visible in Proverbs 1:7 in that Yahweh is the name of God used here. The passage is clear in expressing relationship. Longman writes, "There is no knowledge apart from a proper attitude and relationship to Yahweh."[47]

To use the Tetragrammaton is to use the Lord's covenant name,[48] which demonstrates the strong relational connection to the God of the Torah. The God of wisdom in the Proverbs is the covenant God of the Exodus as well.

> **Nerd Note**
> The *Tetragrammaton* is a certain spelling of the name of God - YHWH (Yahweh). In Proverbs 1:7, Solomon was using the name of God that was connected to his promises to his people. The God who rescued his people from Egypt also gave his people wisdom.

The call to fear Yahweh is connected to his work and care for his people. Sire asks, "What is the meaning of human

---

[46]John Piper, *God Is the Gospel: Meditations on God's Love as the Gift of Himself* (Wheaton, IL: Crossway, 2005), 47.

[47]Longman, *Proverbs,* 100.

[48]Ibid., 101.

history?"[49] in question 7. The answer is relationship with God. Jesus said in John 17:3 that knowing Him is eternal life. Wisdom is relational and wisdom is relationship. The Proverbs are designed to help people live rightly with and before their Lord. Relationship with God is the eternal role that humans were made for and wisdom guides what that relationship should look like.

Solomon offers a contrast in Proverbs 1:7. He shows that the opposite of fearing God is despising wisdom and discipline, which is demonstrative of a relationship problem. Those who fear God recognize how much they do not know compared to Him. To admit that the foolishness of God is wiser than the wisdom of man is not admission of defeat or confession of envy. It should be content for Christian worship—the wise God leads his people. He is on their side (1 Cor 1:25).

God Is the Example

The final question Sire asks is, "What personal, life-orienting core commitments are consistent with this worldview?"[50] Solomon was known as the wisest man who had ever lived and his role in sharing Proverbs was as a teacher. He chose to spend a major portion of his efforts educating others to fear God—to embrace wisdom. In conjunction, God is the epitome of wisdom and He elected to teach people to wisely fear Him. Therefore, Christian teachers should have the core commitment of enacting wisdom by teaching others to be wise as well. In Proverbs, Solomon taught on purity, ethics, money, work ethic, relationships, and much more, but he did not stray from his theme of wisdom.

---

[49]Sire, *The Universe Next Door*, 23.
[50]Sire, *The Universe Next Door*, 23.

Wise teachers work to make wise students. In this sense, biblical integration is wisdom enacted. Can a teacher really teach anything without the beginning of knowledge? No. Teaching must not be informational without being relational as well. If a teacher is to help students live wisely, he must also teach wisely.

Jesus, the greatest teacher, said that the wise listen to his words and put them into practice (Matt 7:24). He said that these people build their homes on the rock. Wise teachers must build on the rock and must encourage students to do the same. The fear of the Lord should be an essential element of every course, unit, and lesson.

Christian education exists to help students listen to the Lord and practice what He has said. It is an investment in helping students be hearers and doers of the Word (Jas 1:22). This type of teaching is a great and pastoral work of wisdom. Understanding which leads to action is what biblical integration is all about and it is an urgent task—time must not be wasted. Psalm 90:12 can teach teachers to make the most of each opportunity by saying, "Teach us to number our days, that we may gain a heart of wisdom." The beginning and heart of wisdom are alike in that God takes the first place in both.

Chapter 3

The Teacher's Priestly Role

SIMPLE SUMMARY
COLOSSIANS 1:15-17 SPEAKS OF CHRIST AS THE REASON FOR AND
GOAL OF CREATION. PRIESTLY TEACHERS HELP STUDENTS
RECOGNIZE THE WORK OF GOD AND RESPOND RIGHTLY TO WHO HE
IS. AS THESE STUDENTS GROW IN RIGHT KNOWLEDGE, THEY MUST
ALSO GROW IN RIGHT THINKING.

The prophetic role of the teacher focuses on truth. It is a rationally and epistemologically driven office. The role of priest is connected, but different. The priest marries the magnificent and metaphysical with the apparent and the relational. Priests represent the mighty God to lowly people and lowly people to the mighty God.[51] Knight explains that this priestly role is especially important because

> the Christian view holds, in opposition to most social theorists, that humanity is not able to solve its own problems, no matter how it manipulates its educational and social environment. The Bible holds that God will intervene in human history a second time to save humanity from itself. That insight, along with a more rounded view of social problems and the condition of human nature, must be taken into consideration in both evaluating

---

[51]John T. Swann, "Priest," in *The Lexham Bible Dictionary*, n.p.

educational theories and in seeking to develop a Christian perspective.[52]

As priests, teachers bring worldview truths to bear on real life issues. The teacher can be an effective prophet by applying the true Christian perspective in a priestly fashion. Educators must not investigate or communicate only either the transcendent or the immanent. They are involved in both because

> **Nerd Note**
> God is *transcendent* because He is over and above.
> God is *immanent* because He is near and involved.

their role is priestly. Wise and priestly rhetoric has enhanced the power and resonance of worldview teaching throughout history for many great teachers, including Old Testament prophets.[53] In the New Testament, Paul continues this priestly tradition by pointing believers to the great High Priest. John Barry suggests that, in Colossians, Paul helps the church grasp that

> God has done what the law, and 'Wisdom,' could not do: sending his own Son in the likeness of sinful flesh, to achieve reconciliation, he dealt with sin on the cross, so that the life which the law had sought to give, the true life of God's people, might be brought to expression in those who, through faith and baptism, belong to Jesus Christ.[54]

---

[52]Knight, *Philosophy & Education*, 142.

[53]Billy K. Smith and Franklin S. Page, *Amos, Obadiah, Jonah*, The New American Commentary, vol. 19B (Nashville: Broadman & Holman, 1995), 30-31.

[54]N. T. Wright, *The Epistles of Paul to the Colossians and to Philemon*, Tyndale New Testament Commentaries (Grand Rapids: Eerdmans, 1986), 39-40.

Colossians 1:15-17

Colossians 1:15-20 is a beautiful poem and a powerful theological decree. Engaging heart and mind, Paul wrote to this young church from prison to tell them "to make Christ the center."[55] Jesus is the Firstborn and Maker, the Connector and Sustainer. He is Lord, whether people choose to honor Him appropriately or not.

All things in, by, and for Him (Col 1:16).

Jesus is the designer and the maker of all things. He is the architect of the visible and invisible. He is the means and end of all things. Colossians 1:16 clearly demonstrates the perfect wisdom of Christ. In fact, Paul directly and purposefully echoes and clarifies the wisdom literature of Proverbs 3:19-20, which says, "By wisdom the Lord laid the earth's foundations, by understanding he set the heavens in place; by his knowledge the watery depths were divided, and the clouds let drop the dew." The syntax of Colossians 1:16 is parallel to that of Proverbs 3:19-20 and, as C. John Collins writes, matches the "divine intellectual attributes of wisdom, understanding, and discernment" to Christ.[56] He is the wisdom that makes the universe make sense. Further, his wisdom holds all things together. Teresa Okure explains,

> He is the ground of being of all creatures in heaven and on earth, visible and invisible, whatever their rank, file or status. All things were created not only in him, but for him. The entire creation belongs to him... Creation originates from God and is

---

[55]John D. Barry, *Colossians: Being Like Jesus*, Not Your Average Bible Study (Bellingham, WA: Lexham, 2014), 21.

[56]C. John Collins, "Colossians 1, 17 'Hold Together': A Co-Opted Term," *Biblica* 95, no. 1 (2014): 84.

executed through and for the Son. He is or
exists before this creation without
exception, and thus ranks before it, as its
irreplaceable ground of being or head,
understood as source.[57]

Beyond being the source, Jesus is the end. According to
Richard Melick, the literal meaning of "for Him" is "unto
Him," which communicates, "Jesus is the goal of all creation.
Everything exists to display his glory, and ultimately he will
be glorified in his creation."[58] All things that are, exist because
of Him.

He is before all things and all things hold together in Him (Col 1:17).

Paul continues by turning the focus to Christ's
preexistence and sustaining power.[59] Yes, He is the beginning
and end, but He is more than that. He is primary and wholly
independent of creation. Melick clarifies, "Since for the
ancients priority in time often meant priority of person, this
argument not only stresses Jesus' role in creating but also
gives him a prominent position with respect to creation."[60]
Paul's means of stressing Christ's prominence is a return to
the Proverbs. The apostle deepened the words of
anthropomorphized Wisdom by connecting them to Christ
Himself in Proverbs 8:23-25:

I was formed long ages ago, at the very
beginning, when the world came to be.

[57]Teresa Okure, "'In Him All Things Hold Together:' A Missiological Reading of Colossians 1:15-20," *International Review of Mission* 91, no. 360 (January 2002): 67.

[58]Richard R. Melick, *Philippians, Colossians, Philemon*, The New American Commentary, vol. 32 (Nashville: Broadman & Holman, 1991), 218.

[59]John Peter Lange et al., *A Commentary on the Holy Scriptures: Colossians* (Bellingham, WA: Logos Bible Software, 2008), 22.

[60]Melick, *Philippians, Colossians, Philemon*, 220.

> When there were no watery depths, I was given birth, when there were no springs overflowing with water; before the mountains were settled in place, before the hills, I was given birth.

Christ is the wisdom that is before all things.[61] Before the mountainous foundations of the earth, there was Jesus. Before the life-giving waters of the world, there was Jesus. But He is not done with the universe. While He was first, He is not finished.

More than just the catalyst for creation, Christ is the engine that keeps it running. It is his power that keeps all things existing and ordered. He has not left or forgotten the work of his hands. He works to sustain and maintain the universe daily.[62] The realities of his identity and activity inform and invite the educator to point to his power and presence through all things. Richard Mouw elaborates,

> Jesus Christ is holding all things together. His integrative mission is a reality even where his authority is not acknowledged. God's intentions for the original creation have not been abandoned. Nor have those intentions been frustrated by the fragmentary features of contemporary life. We can proceed in the confidence that "he shines in all that's fair," even when we do not know exactly how to account for the glimpses of light that we encounter in the darkness.[63]

---

[61]Collins, "Colossians 1, 17," 84.

[62]Melick, *Philippians, Colossians, Philemon*, 220.

[63]Richard J. Mouw, "'In Him All Things Hold Together:' Why God Cares about Ancient Chinese Vases," *Crux* 49, no. 3 (September 2013): 9-10.

Colossians 1:15-17 on Cosmology, Metaphysics, and Relationship

Paul's message to the Colossians came at a crucial time because, as Max Anders says, he was likely battling "a clever company of false teachers who sought to replace the Colossians' enthusiastic devotion to Christ with only a mild approval of him."[64] This challenge is powerful and persuasive. It was as if they were saying, "Do not deny Christ or forget him, but do not make Him too prominent in your thinking either." They taught that Jesus could be powerful, but not preeminent.[65] First-century Colossian Christians were experiencing a challenge to their newly found Christian worldview. According to Douglas Moo, they were "perhaps being tempted to find coherence by pursuing other religious options in their context. In response, Paul wants them to understand that things make sense only when Christ is kept at the center."[66]

Teachers today face the same kinds of worldview struggles. There are myriad theories for where things came from and what they are for. For millennia, the central nature of God in role and identity has been indispensable for faithful biblical integrators. He is to be loved completely, discussed constantly, and shared copiously (Deut 6:4-9). Teachers do not bring the Lord to the center, because He has been there all along, but are responsible to notice,

> **Quick Question**
> What are some of the ways of thinking that tempt students today to try to find meaning and purpose apart from Christ?

[64]Max Anders, *Galatians-Colossians*, Holman New Testament Commentary, vol. 8 (Nashville: Broadman & Holman, 1999), 282.

[65]Ibid., 282-83.

[66]Douglas J. Moo, *The Letters to the Colossians and to Philemon*, Pillar New Testament Commentary (Grand Rapids: Eerdmans, 2008), 126.

affirm, and highlight his presence there. This is their priestly role. Paul taught this way by singing Colossians 1:15-17:

> The Son is the image of the invisible God, the firstborn over all creation. For in him all things were created: things in heaven and on earth, visible and invisible, whether thrones or powers or rulers or authorities; all things have been created through him and for him. He is before all things, and in him all things hold together.

This song likely predates Paul's letter, but was chosen by the apostle to be included because it accurately communicates Christ's relationship to cosmology and metaphysics. Colossians 1:15-17 presents unique material that is central to the Christian's understanding of the universe. Some elements within the refrain are wholly New Testament ideas. In fact, the Old Testament does not speak to God's invisibility or use the term "hold together" concerning the role of God.[67] However, Paul (Rom 1:20; 1 Tim 1:17), along with John (John 1:18, 4:12) and the author of Hebrews (Heb 11:27), highlights these important cosmological and metaphysical realities.

Cosmology is the "study of the universe as an ordered whole."[68] Christianity's cosmology is Christ. Per Jerry Sumney's commentary, Jesus is "the highest being in the cosmos not only because he lived before anything came into being but also because all came into existence through him and continues to exist through his power."[69] This song in Colossians 1 echoes Paul's consistent message that Christ is

[67]Collins, "Colossians 1, 17," 86.

[68]Alan Cairns, *Dictionary of Theological Terms* (Belfast; Greenville, SC: Ambassador Emerald International, 2002), 111.

[69]Jerry L. Sumney, *Colossians: A Commentary*, The New Testament Library (Louisville: Westminster John Knox, 2008), 16.

Creator and Sustainer of all things (Acts 17:24-29; Rom 11:36). This same song should reverberate in the minds and mouths of teachers today. It is the song that students are learning to sing. Since Christ is the cosmological foundation, to teach about anything without regard to Christ is like teaching about human life without reference to conception or birth, or the sustaining actions of the heart or lungs.

Working in conjunction with Christ as cosmological foundation is the reality that He is also the solution to life's metaphysical questions. Cairns writes that metaphysics is "the branch of philosophy that seeks to discover or establish, by means of reason, a general theory of the universe and man's place in it."[70] Metaphysics deals with reasons for how the universe fits together and how mankind fits within it. These types of questions are woven throughout every subject taught in secondary school.

When Paul says that Christ is the "image" of God, he was bringing to mind "likenesses placed on coins, portraits, and for statues."[71] Jesus showed the world exactly who God is. He perfectly represented God to the people. In other words, He executed his priestly role perfectly. However, He also demonstrated that He is Lord over all — "Not only is Jesus the perfect picture of God, but he also holds the highest rank in the universe." [72] Calling Him the "firstborn" is meant to show his rank as most honored, most important, and most prioritized. He is the key figure over all creation.

In Colossians 1:15-17, the identity of Jesus answers the metaphysical questions of the whole universe. He is over all. Everything was created and is sustained through Him. All things are for Him. The whole universe holds together in Him.

The false teaching Paul addressed in Colossae may have been syncretism, mysticism, Gnosticism, Judaism, or

---

[70]Cairns, *Dictionary of Theological Terms*, 278.
[71]Anders, *Galatians-Colossians*, 282-83.
[72]Ibid.

angelic worship.[73] There are many possibilities, but all are attempts at answering key metaphysical questions. Sumney explains that along with reiterating the gospel, Paul presented this song about Christ to the Colossian church to "convince them that the other teaching offers them no spiritual benefit that they do not already possess in Christ."[74]

Knight writes that metaphysics "essentially represents the speculative and synthesizing activities of philosophy, and it provides the theoretical framework that allows scientists and other scholars to create worldviews and develop hypotheses that can be tested according to their basic assumptions."[75] Everyone, whether they recognize it or not, has a framework of understanding through which they interpret the world. In this passage, Paul made it clear that Christ Himself is the ultimate framework. Douglas Moo sums up the key idea: "What holds the universe together is not an idea or a virtue, but a person: the resurrected Christ. Without him, electrons would not continue to circle nuclei, gravity would cease to work, the planets would not stay in their orbits."[76]

Christian educators must never forget that the meaning of life is the Author of Life. Moo writes, "He is the instrument, goal, and sustaining power of the universe."[77] This little hymn is one of the most significant passages describing the Person of Christ.[78] It shows not only who the Lord is, but who all of humanity is in relationship to Him.

---

[73]Sumney, *Colossians*, 10-11.

[74]Sumney, *Colossians*, 12

[75]Knight, *Philosophy & Education*, 16-17.

[76]Moo, *The Letters to the Colossians and to Philemon*, 125-26.

[77]Ibid., 63.

[78]Wright, *The Epistles of Paul to the Colossians and to Philemon*, 64.

He sustains, maintains, orders, and owns. Therefore, no person has existence or identity apart from Christ. All people were made to serve Him and all are his dependents.[79] The Greek ἐν αὐτῷ (in Him) is a locative descriptor. Constantine Campbell states, "All things hold together in the realm or domain of Christ."[80] Humanity and all that humans see and know exists only in Christ. Sumney explains that, clearly, the fact that "the whole cosmos and all the

> **Nerd Note**
> A *locative descriptor* clarifies location. This verse tells us that all things are located within Christ, or are under his control.

beings in it are continually dependent on him for their very existence"[81] should have an impact on the content and purpose of education. This is especially true since Jesus' work is not only a past event, but a current reality. Yes, God has made, but He also currently sustains. Moo writes, "The universe owes its continuing coherence to Christ."[82]

In Colossians 1:20, Paul speaks about Christ, the ultimate metaphysical answer, seeking reconciliation with all people and things. Since the answer to life's metaphysical questions is a Person, relationship with that Person is essential. Therefore, the priestly role of the teacher flows directly from the prophetic. It is not enough to share truth with students without leading them to a right response. Paul called the Colossian church to make Christ the center[83] and he was pleading with them to elevate Jesus in their lives to the place He already occupies in the universe at large.

---

[79]Ibid., 73.

[80]Constantine R. Campbell, *Colossians and Philemon: A Handbook on the Greek Text* (Waco, TX: Baylor University Press, 2013), 13.

[81]Sumney, *Colossians*, 70.

[82]Moo, *The Letters to the Colossians and to Philemon*, 125.

[83]Barry, *Colossians*, 21.

The integrating teacher is a redemptive and reconciling teacher. This kind of teacher allows all course content to herald the ambassador's call — come back to God (2 Cor 5:20). The goal of the priestly teacher is to represent God to the students through every piece of information, every question, and every discovery. All things are held together in Him. He is before all things. He is meant to be first and foremost. The teacher who embraces the role of priest makes academic curriculum an instrument through which to play the song Paul sang to the Colossians.

Chapter 4

The Teacher's Kingly Role

SIMPLE SUMMARY
PSALM 19 SHOWS THAT GOD'S WORLD AND GOD'S WORD SPEAK
ABOUT HIM. AS TEACHERS, WE MUST USE BOTH OF THESE TOOLS TO
HELP OUR STUDENTS UNDERSTAND WHAT IS TRUE AND WHAT IS
WORTH LIVING FOR. WHEN WE SHOW THEM WHAT IS RIGHT AND
GOOD, WE ARE EMBRACING THE TEACHER'S KINGLY ROLE.

John T. Swann shares that in the Old Testament, "The priesthood and monarchy were inexorably connected. It was the king's duty to enforce and uphold the covenantal obligations, and the priesthood's instruction was vital to that duty."[84] The same is true concerning the roles of Christian teachers in the classroom today. The priestly teacher pictures and points to Christ and his glory. The kingly teacher calls students to value and follow that glorious Christ. The teacher must be a good leader—a "king" who wields power and leadership for the benefit of the class's citizens.

Two fields of educational philosophy undergird the kingly teacher's role—epistemology and axiology. Norman Geisler introduces epistemology as "the discipline that deals with theory of knowledge."[85] Epistemology is concerned with how people can know things—what is true and what is truth?

Empiricism is a framework which holds that knowledge can be gained through the senses.[86] Empiricism is related to science in that it focuses on what can be seen, heard,

---

[84]Swann, "Priest."

[85]Norman L. Geisler, "Epistemology," in *Baker Encyclopedia of Christian Apologetics*, Baker Reference Library (Grand Rapids: Baker, 1999), 215.

[86]Knight, *Philosophy & Education*, 22.

40

smelled, tasted, and felt. Theologians refer to this kind of knowledge as general revelation. It is widely available to all who will pay attention. Empiricism is a major intellectual force today and has been for millennia. George Knight explains,

> Empirical knowledge is built into the very nature of human experience. Individuals may walk out of doors on a spring day and see the beauty of the landscape, hear the song of a bird, feel the warm rays of the sun, and smell the fragrance of the blossoms. They "know" that it is spring because of the messages received through their senses. This knowledge is composed of ideas formed in accordance with observed data. Sensory knowing among humans is immediate and universal, and in many ways it forms the basis for much of our knowledge.[87]

In addition to empiricism, Christians must understand the role of direct revelation in grasping truth. J. I. Packer declares that Christianity "rests on revelation: nobody would know the truth about God, or be able to relate to him in a personal way, had not God first acted to make himself known."[88] What God has specifically and directly shared through his Scripture is known as special revelation. Knight speaks to this as well:

> Revealed knowledge has been of prime importance in the field of religion. It differs from all other sources of knowledge by

[87]Ibid.

[88]J. I. Packer, *Concise Theology: A Guide to Historic Christian Beliefs* (Wheaton, IL: Tyndale, 1993).

> presupposing a transcendent supernatural reality that breaks into the natural order. Revelation is God's communication concerning the divine will. Believers in revelation hold that this form of knowledge has the distinct advantage of being an omniscient source of information that is not obtainable through other epistemological methods. The truth gained through this source is believed to be absolute and uncontaminated.[89]

Thankfully, God has chosen to speak to mankind through both special and general revelation. However, his message is not only focused on information, but on transformation. God cares that his people know and value Him. Just as epistemology is about knowing, axiology is about valuing.

What is of value? What is most desirable? What is worth pursuing? Axiology interacts with some of these questions. People are motivated by what they value and different value systems create different views of the good life.[90] When people view wealth, comfort, relationship, power, or reputation as ultimately valuable, that will direct their lives to pursue those things. Personal axiology is what drives choices, goals, dreams, habits, and visions of success.

These two fields of philosophy are important to the kingly role of the teacher. Kings must lead from and toward real truth and value if they are to be successful leaders. For example, epistemology will affect curricular development in the Christian school because of the presupposition of the existence of God and authority of the Bible.[91] Axiology is similarly important in the teacher's kingly role. Knight writes

[89]Knight, *Philosophy & Education*, 23.
[90]Ibid., 28.
[91]Knight, *Philosophy & Education*, 26-27.

that the actions and attitudes of teachers "constantly instruct groups of highly impressionable young people who assimilate and imitate their teachers' value structures to a significant extent."[92] What the teacher loves and hates, values and disregards, will impact citizens of the class.

Psalm 19

Psalm 19 is a magnificent poem that speaks directly to Christian epistemology and axiology. C. S. Lewis called it "the greatest poem in the Psalter and one of the greatest lyrics in the world."[93] It is beautiful and bountiful—lifting the reader's mind to see and sing with the psalmist. The psalm can be divided into three complimentary parts. Verses 1-6 focus on God's general revelation in creation, verses 7-10 point out God's special revelation in his Law, and verses 11-14 focus on the response of the servant.[94]

> **Quick Question**
> Do you think that what you love/hate impacts the class? Why or why not?

The heavens declare (vv. 1-6).

All that has been created shouts the glory of God. Every person experiences the language of creation. John Calvin describes the work of creation:

> The heavens have a common language to teach all men without distinction, nor is there any thing but their own carelessness to hinder even those who are most strange

---

[92]Ibid., 29.

[93]C. S. Lewis, *Reflections on the Psalms* (Orlando: Harcourt, 1958), 63.

[94]Nancy Declaisse-Walford, Rolf A. Jacobson, and Beth Laneel Tanner, *The Book of Psalms*, The New International Commentary on the Old Testament (Grand Rapids: Eerdmans, 2014), 203.

to each other, and who live in the most distant parts of the world, from profiting, as it were, at the mouth of the same teacher.[95]

If people truly paid attention to the voice of creation, they would learn the reality and magnificence of the Lord. Even one day beneath the sky, or one night under the stars, should be enough to for all people to clearly hear the teacher's testimony.[96] However, people do not all pay attention.

While nature shouts God's praise, James Smith explains one issue: "The message of the heavenly bodies is real, but it is inarticulate."[97] The heavens do not speak with words in the ways humans do. They make their case powerfully, but they do not make their case in human language.[98]

The Law gives life (vv. 7-10).

Calvin spoke also to the unique need for God's Law: "While the heavens bear witness concerning God, their testimony does not lead men so far as that thereby they learn truly to fear him, and acquire a well-grounded knowledge of him; it serves only to render them inexcusable."[99] The Word of God is a more direct and clear messenger of God. It is not present in the same way as creation, but it is a more wonderful gift.

James Smith describes the Law of God as perfect: "Flawless, without defect or error; a guide which can neither mislead nor fail. . . . Like food for the hungry, the law can

[95]John Calvin and James Anderson, *Commentary on the Book of Psalms* (Bellingham, WA: Logos Bible Software, 2010), 1:312.

[96]Calvin and Anderson, *Commentary on the Book of Psalms*, 1:310.

[97]James E. Smith, *The Wisdom Literature and Psalms*, Old Testament Survey Series (Joplin, MO: College Press Pub. Co., 1996), Ps 19:3.

[98]Robert G. Bratcher and William David Reyburn, *A Translator's Handbook on the Book of Psalms*, UBS Handbook Series (New York: United Bible Societies, 1991), 190.

[99]Calvin and Anderson, *Commentary on the Book of Psalms*, 1:317.

refresh and restore the soul."[100] While nature can reveal man's need, Scripture can meet that need. This is not to say that they are at odds; rather, the Word of God works in partnership with creation.

The Law has four effects on those who obey it — revival for the soul, wisdom for the simple, joy for the heart, and light for the eyes.[101] God's Word provides the powerful wisdom that comes from fearing the Lord. The Word, in conjunction with the world, brings life.

Wisdom is knowing and pleasing God (vv. 11-14).

The way in which people access real life is through relationship with God Himself. Creation and Scripture point those who will listen toward the Person of God. When awe meets law and the reality of God is encountered, the attentive person turns to God for help. The awesomeness of God invites man to come and bring his weakness to the Lord for help.[102]

In Psalm 19:14, the psalmist ends his song by asking that God would turn his words and thoughts from foolishness to wisdom. He wants his life to bring pleasure to the Lord.[103] His experience in God's world and God's Word has transformed him. The knowledge that he has gained has changed his aims. Upon seeing and knowing God, he now values Him most.

> **Quick Question**
> How can your class content, and the way you present it, help students move from foolishness to wisdom? How can it be leveraged to help students honor God?

---

[100]Smith, *The Wisdom Literature and Psalms*, Ps 19:7.

[101]Bratcher and Reyburn, *A Translator's Handbook*, 193.

[102]Smith, *The Wisdom Literature and Psalms*, Ps 19:12-13.

[103]Bratcher and Reyburn, *A Translator's Handbook*, 196.

Psalm 19 on Epistemology and Axiology

Psalm 19 flows from epistemology to axiology in such a seamless fashion that it could be used as an exemplar of biblical integration. The world speaks truth and then the Word speaks truth. There is a marriage between the scientific observation of the heavens and the devotional investigation of the Bible. These actions do not lead to knowledge alone, but naturally flow into a response of worship — ascribing worth to God. The Christian educator functions in a kingly role, much like David in Psalm 19, by helping students pay attention to reality and respond rightly.

Gerstenberger identifies that axiological and epistemological intention of Psalm 19: "Adoration of Yahweh and meditative prayer encouraged the discovery of individual identity within the community of faith."[104] This same goal is held by Christian educators. Teachers aim to allow God's world and God's Word to shape the individual. The realities of God, displayed in verses 1-10, demand the personal response displayed in verses 11-14. The truth, or epistemology, motivates valuing, or axiology. This kind of impact is the reason for Christian education.

The way that truth leads value is apparent in Psalm 19. During the first part of the psalm, which highlights God's glory in creation, the Hebrew word for God is *El*. However, the name *Yahweh* is used in the next part of the psalm as it speaks of God's Law. Robert Good explains that *El* is a "generic word for 'god' in the ancient Semitic languages,"[105] but, as Mark Powell writes, *Yahweh* is "the most important name for God in the Hebrew Bible." [106] It is the Tetragrammaton that, as was mentioned previously, is God's

---

[104]Erhard S. Gersternberger, *Psalms*, pt. 1, The Forms of Old Testament Literature, vol. 14 (Grand Rapids: Eerdmans, 1988), 103.

[105]Robert M. Good, "El," in *The HarperCollins Bible Dictionary*, ed. Mark Allan Powell, rev. ed. (New York: HarperCollins, 2011), 228.

[106]Mark Allan Powell, "Yahweh," in *The HarperCollins Bible Dictionary*, 1118.

covenant name. The use of Yahweh denotes personal relationship. Therefore, it should be noted that Psalm 19 moves from speaking of "the God" to "my God." The truth about his glory and invisible attributes is made clear by creation (Rom 1:20). Creation tells about Him. However, in his Word, He speaks for Himself. Nancy Declaisse-Walford challenges readers:

> Just imagine, after all, what kind of a god Israel would have worshipped if all they knew of God had had to deduce from earthquakes and floods; predators and prey; sun, rain and seasons. In creation, the Creator comes to us hidden, wearing nature as a mask. In the word, the Lord (Yahweh) comes to us personally. Here, we meet a God who is gracious and merciful, slow to anger, abounding in steadfast love, showing faithfulness to the thousandth generation.[107]

There is no way for teachers to rightly exercise their kingly roles of leading their classes without looking to the King of kings. Biblical integration is made possible by grounding truth on the empirical knowledge of the world and the revealed knowledge of the Word. In the world, God's greatness is apparent. In the Word, it is articulated. A biblical epistemology will lead to biblical axiology. Teachers show students what to love

> **Practical Point**
> We are not just leading our students to know, but also to love. We must be showing them what is and is not worth living for. This takes intentional effort and care.

---

[107]Declaisse-Walford, Jacobson, and Tanner, *The Book of Psalms*, 213.

and value as they share knowledge. Psalm 19 brings the marriage of empirical and moral truth to the forefront. It binds general and special revelation together. Biblical integrators do the same.

Conclusion

William Yount writes, "Pastor-teachers are shepherds who nurture their flocks, feed their flocks, protect their flocks. Pastor-teachers are also instructors who train, prepare, and equip the sheep of the Lord."[108] Christian teachers are pastors and they have a serious responsibility. Yount explains that there is a dangerous tendency to slide into "teaching subjects more than teaching students."[109] It is important for teachers to see students as their *mathetes*, which is the Greek word for apprentices or disciples.[110] The pastoral role of the educator is to teach the heart, head, and hands to know and honor God in all things. This means serving in a prophetic, priestly, and kingly fashion for the good of the student and the glory of God.

---

[108]Yount, *Called to Teach*, 228.

[109]Ibid., 229.

[110]Ibid.

PART TWO

THE THEORETICAL, PRACTICAL, AND HISTORICAL BASIS FOR BIBLICAL INTEGRATION

Speaking to teachers, Christian education authority Howard Hendricks issued the challenge, "Wake up to the realization that each day you can give the Lord of your life even greater control over your being."[111] In addition, in his foreword to Mark Eckel's *The Whole Truth*, worldview expert Chuck Colson called Eckel's biblical integration strategies "a great weapon in training young minds to engage the culture with discernment and a well-grounded biblical view of life."[112] Part Two is designed to help committed Christian educators awaken to a passion to give God greater control of their teaching through the skillful wielding of the weapon of biblical integration. Biblical integration is the necessary reconstruction of educational connections that have been artificially severed. Speaking of marriage and divorce, Jesus said, "What God has joined together, let no one separate" (Mark 10:9). The educational culture has divorced Christianity from learning in many areas and in many ways. This section assists educators by making the case for reconciliation and addressing key areas to be reunited—heart and mind, general and special revelation, word and deed.

---

[111]Howard Hendricks, *Teaching to Change Lives* (Colorado Springs: Multnomah, 1987), 25.

[112]Chuck Colson, foreword to *The Whole Truth: Classroom Strategies for Biblical Integration*, by Mark Eckel (Maitland, FL: Xulon, 2003), vi.

Chapter Five

What Makes Education Distinctly Christian?

SIMPLE SUMMARY
CHRISTIAN EDUCATION IS MORE THAN TRADITIONAL TEACHING
WITH THE ADDITION OF CHAPEL SERVICES, PRAYER BEFORE CLASS,
OR BIBLE COURSES. ALL CONTENT MUST BE TAUGHT FROM AND
TOWARD THE REALITIES OF GOD. BIBLICAL INTEGRATION IS NOT
TYING THEOLOGY INTO COURSEWORK. RATHER, IT IS BRINGING OUT
THE CONNECTIONS THAT ARE ALREADY THERE.

Christian schooling is not a new phenomenon. God-centered education has been a priority for the Lord's people for millennia. After rescuing the Israelites from Egypt, God called his people to keep his commands on their hearts and lips (Deut 6:6-9). He told parents to impress his commands and characteristics on their children, to weave them into every conversation, and to connect them to life at home and in the community. Throughout the ages, educational practice has changed in many ways, but Christians still see the importance of a distinctly Christian education. Believers still want to write God's character and commands onto and into every area of life. In current time and contemporary school culture, there is need for a robust practice of biblical integration.

In 1957, Donald Oppewal, education professor at Calvin College, championed the need for biblical integration by saying that all courses taught at a Christian school should be "required to show their credentials before being allowed into a curriculum which dares to call itself Christian. . . . They will be admitted only insofar as they are able to be used as an avenue of revelation."[113] He went on to say that to teach any content apart from pointing to the Person and glory of God is to engage in "riotous teaching" and the selling of "our distinctive educational birthright for a mess of pottage."[114] Educators called to teach in Christian schools are called to Christ-centered instruction. To practice anything else is to make an unworthy exchange.

The conversation advanced further as the aim of integration continued to be clarified when, in 1968, Francis Schaeffer got to the heart of integrated thinking:

> True education means thinking by associating across various disciplines, not just being highly qualified in one field, as a technician might be. I suppose that no discipline has tended to think in a more fragmented fashion than the orthodox or evangelical theology of today.[115]

He noticed that even in institutions holding to Christian values, Christianity had been removed, or had removed itself, from much of academic discussion. This separation is what Oppewal said causes Christian educators' "repeated insistence upon the distinctiveness of Christian education" to become a lie.[116] Truly Christian education requires transdisciplinary engagement of theological nature and substance.

Quick Question
How confident are you in your ability to practice truly Christian teaching?

---

[113]Donald Oppewal, "Toward a Distinctive Curriculum for Christian Education," *Reformed Journal* 7, no. 8 (September 1957): 24.

[114]Ibid.

[115]Francis Schaeffer, *The Francis A. Schaeffer Trilogy: Three Essential Books in One Volume.* (Wheaton, IL: Crossway, 1990), 12.

[116]Oppewal, "Toward a Distinctive Curriculum," 21.

More recently, George Knight notes the continuation of this trend of disengagement: "All too often, Christian education has not been deliberately built upon a distinctive Christian philosophy. As a result, many Christian schools have tended to offer something less than Christian education and have thereby frustrated the purpose of their existence."[117] The key to overcoming this frustration is the practice of coherent and cogent biblical integration.

Like Christian schools, the local church is also currently struggling in her efforts to educate young people effectively.[118] The goal of mentioning these educational struggles is not to diminish the role and value of the local church, but to partner with her and serve her in the important pastoral role of teaching. One representative area of weakness is Sunday school. Todd Hillard, Britt Beemer, and Ken Ham write that in a 2009 survey of the effects of Sunday school it was discovered, "Sunday school is actually more likely to be detrimental to the spiritual and moral health of our children."[119] That statement is stunning, but the survey research of 1,000 young people in their 20s bears out that those who regularly attended Sunday school in middle and high school are

- more likely NOT to believe that all the accounts/stories in the Bible are true/accurate.
- more likely to doubt the Bible because it was written by men.
- more likely to doubt the Bible because it was not translated correctly.
- more likely to defend that abortion should continue to be legal.
- more likely to defend premarital sex.

[117]George R. Knight, *Philosophy & Education: An Introduction in Christian Perspective*, 4th ed. (Berrien Springs, MI: Andrews University Press, 2006), 165.

[118]Todd Hillard, Britt Beemer, and Ken Ham, *Already Gone: Why Your Kids Will Quit Church and What You Can Do to Stop It* (Green Forest, AR: Master Books, 2009), locs. 420-22, Kindle.

[119]Ibid., locs. 397-400.

- more likely to accept that gay marriage and abortion
  should be legal . . .
- more likely to view the Church as hypocritical.
- much more likely to have become anti-church through
  the years.
- more likely to believe that good people don't need to
  go to church.[120]

How can it be that consistent Christian education of
teens is not bearing, but instead, killing fruit? Hillard, Beemer,
and Ham share, "The numbers indicate that Sunday school
actually didn't do anything to help them develop a Christian
worldview. . . . As shocking as this sounds, the reality we
have to face is that Sunday school clearly harmed the spiritual
growth of the kids."[121] Clearly, Bible knowledge is not the
same as biblical worldview thinking.

John Frame defines theology as "the application of
Scripture, by persons, to all areas of life."[122] He goes on to say
that the goal of teaching is "to bring spiritual health to its
hearers."[123] Christian school educators have the opportunity
to help develop Christian worldview thinking in young
people by teaching them to apply Scripture to all areas of life.
This can be done effectively because school teachers are
already speaking to many of the most significant areas of life.

The timing of primary, middle, and secondary
education is also a key element. This a time of identity and
cognitive development. This time of life is more crucial in
worldview formation than the years devoted to higher
education. Christian colleges often cannot effectively impact
students to overcome a non-integrated secondary education.
Beemer, a Christian leader and expert in consumer behavior,
writes of the value of Christian colleges: "If parents knew the

---

[120]Hillard, Beemer, and Ham, *Already Gone*, locs. 404-10.

[121]Ibid., loc. 435-37.

[122]John Frame, *John Frame's Selected Shorter Writings* (Phillipsburg, NJ: P & R,
2015), 2:69.

[123]Ibid., 2:70.

truth, they would, in most instances, probably put their money somewhere else."[124] He goes on to share that numerous studies show negligible impact of Christian colleges on students knowing, loving, and following God. The conclusion he presents is, "If we are going to stop the epidemic, it needs to happen in the Church and in the home during the elementary, middle school, and high school years."[125]

The key to overcoming this frustration, in the church and school, is the practice of coherent and cogent biblical integration. This interconnected teaching will lead to right thinking—deep understanding that all things are built on the foundational reality of God and that all things exist for the glory of God. This integration is the essential element to Christian education. There can be no Christian education without recognizing the centrality of Christ in all things because He is central and supreme in all things. John Piper makes the case that this truth is foundational to Christian educational identity:

> Christ not only made and owns the world, he not only holds everything together by the word of his power, but he also created it and sustains it to display his beauty and his worth and greatness so that those whom he created in his image will know him and treasure him above all things, and in that treasuring of him above all that he has made, manifest his supreme value in the universe. . . . All things not only belong to Christ, but all things display Christ. Human beings exist to magnify his worth in the world. Our worth consists of our

---

[124]Hillard, Beemer, and Ham, *Already Gone*, locs. 1097-98.

[125]Hillard, Beemer, and Ham, *Already Gone*, locs. 1102-3.

capacity to consciously make much of his worth.[126]

A Class Is a Worldview Tool

Since all things are from, for, and to Him, educators must teach all things as from, to, and for Him. This does not mean that every class becomes a Bible class. Instead, each course is restored to its intended purpose—teaching content to magnify the Lord. The worldview survey textbook *Understanding the Times* by Jeff Myers and David A. Noebel is an enduring example of what integration can look like in a number of content areas.[127] This book is recognized by evangelical leaders as one of the finest tools available in helping students think Christianly.[128] How does this text accomplish this task so effectively? Rather than replacing course content with Christian content, it investigates theology, philosophy, ethics, biology, psychology, sociology, law, politics, economics, and history from a variety of worldviews. These subjects are "ten ways of looking at the world,"[129] and by examining each of them from a variety of vantage points, the superiority and validity of Christianity is made apparent. In other words, by reuniting these ten crucial subjects with the Christian worldview, right thinking results. The truth and value of Christian thinking is magnified by the way the book presents the contrasting commitments of other major ways of thinking.

---

[126]John Piper, *Think: The Life of the Mind and the Love of God* (Wheaton, IL: Crossway, 2010), locs. 2623-34, Kindle.

[127]Jeff Myers and David A. Noebel, *Understanding the Time: A Survey of Competing Worldviews* (Manitou Springs, CO: Summit Ministries, 2015).

[128]Summit, "Hear What the Experts Are Saying," accessed February 11, 2017, http://understandingthetimes.com/testimonials/.

[129]James Thornton, "Controlling Culture Currents," *New American* 31 (December 2015): 29.

Each course taught in a Christian school is a kind of magnifying glass that zooms in on a particular area. That area is investigated and understood so that the students can learn to know, worship, and love God more fully. For example, a biology course zooms in on the study of life and this must, in turn, put the focus on the Author of life. *Understanding the Times* has been praised since its first edition because it "provides fair and accurate exposition of thinkers so that they might speak for themselves, and it then proceeds to unpack their systems for the high-school and/or college student to consider in his or her own mind."[130] What Myers and Noebel accomplish in their book is the same thing that every Christian educator is striving to accomplish in their classrooms and curricula. The teacher presents the content with the goal of allowing the students to apprehend the reality, magnificence, and care of the Lord. This teaching methodology is not an overbearing indoctrination, but an invitation to honest acceptance of God and his ways. Teachers must walk with students through the process of learning God as they learn their subjects.

Joshua Reichard proposes that integrating teachers coach students through the steps of conflict, creativity, and commitment: "The conflict stage occurs in a faith-affirming environment where students are free to ask difficult questions and wrestle with difficult problems."[131] There must be space for students to be honest and open. Like a swimming instructor, a teacher needs to let the students work, but with the confidence that they will never be in danger of drowning. Teachers are not called to answer or explain away every hard question for the students. In fact, they may not fully

---

[130]John S. Reist, Jr., "Understanding the Times: The Story of the Biblical Christian, Marxist/ Leninist, and Secular Humanist Worldviews," *Journal of the Evangelical Theological Society* 38, no. 1 (March 1995): 139.

[131]Joshua D. Reichard, "From Indoctrination to Initiation: A Non-Coercive Approach to Faith-Learning Integration," *Journal of Education & Christian Belief* 17, no. 2 (October 2013): 292.

understand the issues either. However, in the same way that swimming instructors do not hold students up every time they try to swim a lap, teachers provide a safe place for students to struggle with information, commitments, outcomes, and ideas. This safe struggle leads to growth in strength, ability, and confidence.

The creativity stage comes next. In this area, teachers offer opportunity for students to work through the conflict. However, the teacher is not disengaged in this activity. Reichard explains that, here, the teacher must facilitate "the exploration of beliefs and values, but at the same time, reinforce the distinctions between the Christian faith and 'society at large.'"[132] The swimming instructor does not leave the student to flail in the water, nor does he carry the student across the water. Instead, he sets an example or encourages the student to employ specific techniques in helpful ways.

Success in the creativity stage leads to the final stage: commitment. By allowing students to ask questions and work to find solutions in a safe and supported environment, the teacher is offering opportunities for students to discover the superiority and value of Christianity for themselves. They are developing their own Christian identity. Concerning these three steps, Reichard concludes, "Initiation allows students to struggle with their faith, but then immediately to formulate solutions and apply it to life and learning."[133]

Biblically integrated teaching is about much more than information. It is about a journey. The teacher is building the curriculum on worldview commitments and leading students toward those commitments. Teachers work with their students in engaging and exploring, noticing and negotiating, inviting conversation and seeking illumination. The purpose of the journey is not to indoctrinate students into Christianity

---

[132]Ibid.

[133]Reichard, "From Indoctrination to Initiation," 293.

by creating theological connections, but to help them see and wrestle with the interconnectivity that already exists.

With gentleness and respect, teachers revere Christ and tenderly help students discover answers for the hope within them (1 Pet 3:15). In the learning environment, Christian thinking trumps Christian knowing. Rather than indoctrination, biblical integration should be an invitation to, an explanation of, an ongoing conversation about, and a demonstration of Christianity.

Biblical Integration Is Unique

In an increasingly diverse culture, numerous worldviews and ideologies claim to be the way, truth, and life. Myers and Noebel write,

> If you look in the religion section of a bookstore you'll see books on Christianity and Islam, of course, but also on Confucianism, Buddhism, Taoism, Hinduism, Vedantism, Jainism, Shintoism, and many others. Each religion attempts to explain what the world is like and how we should live.[134]

---

[134]Myers and Noebel, *Understanding the Times*, 7.

There is an increasing interest in secular and naturalistic worldviews. The journey of trying to grow in understanding the world can be undertaken through any number of presuppositional roads, but there is only one accurate worldview. In Matthew 7, Jesus explained to his listeners that there are bad roads, false teachers, counterfeit disciples, and weak foundations. Christian educators have the chance to cultivate true disciples by leading them on the narrow road and building on the rock. Along with being a meaningful opportunity, teaching is a significant responsibility that must be taken up with seriousness and thoughtfulness.

> **Nerd Note**
> Islam, Confucianism, Buddhism, Taoism, Hinduism, Vedantism, Jainism, and Shintoism are examples of other religious worldviews.
>
> ---
>
> *Presuppositions* are the foundational ideas that people have. We build all of our other learning on presuppositions. These can be religious beliefs or other ideas about how the world works. Many people do not recognize their presuppositions, but they are still influential.

Kevin D. Miller, Professor of Communication at Huntington University, tells of a personal experience as an instructor that is helpful in working through what makes distinctly biblical integration unique. While moving toward tenure at his university, he was required to write a "faith-learning integration" paper.[135] While this is a normal practice in many Christian educational institutions, he wondered how he should think of a Muslim professor who was his counterpart at an Islamic school integrating non-Christian faith and learning:

---

[135] Other Christians might call this a biblical integration paper or a Philosophy of Christian Education paper.

Should I hope he succeeds brilliantly, or
that he fundamentally fails since his frame
of reference is ultimately heretical and
flawed? If we both succeed, what do the
efforts tell us about exercise of integration
of faith and learning and the disciplinary
truths of the world we are able to fit
conceptually into our respective
metaphysic convictions?[136]

Miller found the solution to his questions in the
example and identity of Christ. Jesus did not coerce people
into believing, but worked through "the skillful drawing out
and maturing of knowledge in the student."[137] Biblical
integration is not only bringing truth from the outside in, but
also from the inside out. Jesus is Lord. He is Savior. He is
Creator. These are facts. Christianity is not an ingredient to be
added in, but a very present flavor and aroma that should be
drawn out. The reality that religious facts are challenged does
not reduce their truthfulness. This is the where the difference
between Christian and all other types of integration must be
noted.

A Christian teacher is not beholden to his ability to
bring theology into any topic. God already ordained that He
should be glorified by that idea, object, or phenomenon. Any
intelligent person can force the synthesis of two ideas. This
forced relationship occurs not only with various religious
faiths built on the supernatural, but with those committed to a
naturalistic worldview as well. However, Christian worldview
integration is not synthetic but paradigmatic.[138] It is not about

---

[136]Kevin D. Miller, "Reframing the Faith-Learning Relationship: Bonhoeffer and an Incarnational Alternative to the Integration Model," *Christian Scholar's Review* 43, no. 2 (Winter 2014): 132.

[137]Ibid., 133.

[138]James R. Estep, "What Makes Education Christian?" in *A Theology for Christian Education*, by James R. Estep, Michael J. Anthony, and Gregg R. Allison (Nashville: B & H, 2008), 34.

adding one thing to another, but understanding truth by truth: observing the connections God has made. The general revelation of God's world is designed as connected to the special revelation of God's Word. Teachers do not need to invent

> **Nerd Note**
> Something is *synthetic* when it combines two or more ingredients. A *paradigm* is an overarching way of looking at something. Biblical integration is *paradigmatic* because it is done by trying to see the world as God does.

connections because they already exist.

Bradley McKoy, a physics professor at Asuza Pacific University, explains that a class should engage in "theologically informed reflection on academic disciplines and, reciprocally, reflection on theology and faith practice in light of discipline-specific learning."[139] The Christian physics teacher brings theology to bear on science, but also brings a scientific understanding to his theology. The theology deepens the science and the science deepens the theology. Oppewal explains by saying that if a young child and an experienced physicist observe a thunderstorm, they both see the heavens declaring the glory of God through the same event (Ps 19:1). However, their experiences are vastly different:

> The physicist sees God in the workings of the thunderstorm, while the child experiences only light, noise, and dampness. The child's vision of God's power and might is hampered by his lack of insight into the pattern, the system, the structure of weather. To the extent that he sees and experiences no laws or is aware of

---

[139]Bradley K. McCoy, "Developing a Program-Level Faith Integration Curriculum: A Case Study from Physics," *Christian Higher Education* 13, no. 5 (December 2014): 340-41.

no pattern, he knows not God in general revelation.[140]

Biblical integration must be practiced to grow students from worshiping the God of light and noise into students worshiping the God of weather. As they learn Christ's world, they will better learn Christ and their love and awe will be deepened. Consider the experience of the disciples in Matthew 8. Jesus spoke to the storm and brought calm to the tempest (v. 26). The disciples responded with awe and fear, saying, "What kind of man is this? Even the winds and the waves obey him!" (v. 37; Mark 4:41). Their amazement for God was enhanced because of their fisherman's knowledge of waters and winds. Their knowledge of the general revelation enhanced the power they saw in Christ's command. In the same way, Peter responded with worship and recognition of his own sin when Jesus performed the miracle of providing an unbelievable catch of fish in Luke 5:8. Peter knew about catching fish and his expertise in that area enhanced his awe at the power of Jesus.

Therefore, the superiority of Christian education and biblical integration does not exist because Christian teachers are better instructors than others. It does not exist because of better academic content or a more passionate zeal for the needs of society. It exists because the God of Christianity is superior.[141] He is real, and He desires to be known.

[140]Oppewal, "Toward a Distinctive Curriculum," 23.
[141]Estep, "What Makes Education Christian?," 34.

Chapter 6

Understanding Biblical Integration

SIMPLE SUMMARY

BIBLICAL INTEGRATION INCLUDES TEARING DOWN ARTIFICIAL
DIVISIONS BETWEEN HEART AND MIND, GENERAL AND SPECIAL
REVELATION, AND WORD AND DEED.

John Piper is widely considered "one of the most important pastor theologians of our time."[142] He has been a pastoral, missional, and theological leader for the evangelical church for decades. While trained at seminary and the university, it was high school geometry and advanced biology that awakened his "love for right thinking."[143] The skills that have borne much fruit in his life, and for the life of the church, were born in high school science and math.

Spiritual development is the task of all Christian educators regardless of academic discipline because all reality points to the God who made and maintains it. James R. Nichols, professor and chair of the Department of Biology at Abilene Christian University, affirms the teacher's role in discipleship:

> As a Christian academic, regardless of my academic discipline, I am in the business of spiritual formation and soul care with my students. It is not sufficient for me to be simply a biology professor. It is not sufficient for me to be simply an educator,

[142]John Piper, "The Collected Works of John Piper," accessed December 7, 2016, https://www.crossway.org/books/the-collected-works-of-john-piper-hconly/.

[143]John Piper and D. A. Carson, *The Pastor as Scholar and the Scholar as Pastor: Reflections on Life and Ministry* (Wheaton, IL: Crossway, 2011), 27.

> even an effective educator. Somehow I
> must include aspects of my instruction,
> guidance, and mentoring that surpass the
> academic discipline and reach into the
> eternal, even if only in a barely perceptible
> amount.[144]

Nichols is describing the task of biblical integration. As Kenneth Badley points out, there is currently some disagreement concerning the identity and practice of biblical integration because its "component words—faith, learning, and integration—all carry several potential meanings."[145] Perry L. Glanzer, a professor in Baylor University's School of Education, believes that the language of integration should be discarded in favor of terms like the "creation and redemption of scholarship."[146] These new terms emphasize "the broad, positive theological work in which Christian academics should engage."[147] The goal here is not to fight a semantic battle, but to point out that the true nature of biblical integration is redemptive and constructive. Karl Bailey clarifies that the call of Christian educators is to "redeem and reconstruct" their teaching in light of the truths of Christianity.[148] Therefore, biblical integration should be seen as the unification of truths. It is the restoration of relationship between heart and mind, special revelation and general revelation, and word and deed. It is a tearing down of the

---

[144]James R. Nichols, "The Science Professor as Pastor," *Perspectives on Science and Christian Faith* 64, no. 4 (December 2012): 251.

[145]Kenneth Rea Badley, "Clarifying 'Faith-Learning Integration': Essentially Contested Concepts and the Concept-Conception Distinction," *Journal of Education and Christian Belief Spring* 13, no. 1 (April 2009): 7.

[146]Perry L. Glanzer, "Why We Should Discard 'the Integration of Faith and Learning'": Rearticulating the Mission of the Christian Scholar," *Journal of Education & Christian Belief* 12, no. 1 (Spring 2008): 43.

[147]Ibid., 45.

[148]Karl G. D. Bailey, "Faith-Learning Integration, Critical Thinking Skills, and Student Development in Christian Education," *Journal of Research on Christian Education* 21, no. 2 (August 2012): 153.

artificial divisions, which starts with the bringing together of the heart and mind.

Heart and Mind (The Aim)

Worldview expert Nancy Pearcey communicates, "The first step in forming a Christian worldview is to overcome this sharp divide between 'heart' and 'brain.'"[149] In current culture, facts and values have been separated in an unnatural fashion so that the truth of the gospel has been relegated to the realm of personal opinion and perspective rather than being considered an objective truth claim. Pearcey continues, "God is not just the Savior of souls, He is also the Lord of creation. One way we acknowledge His Lordship is by interpreting every aspect of creation in light of His truth."[150] This reuniting of truth with truth is one part of what makes education truly Christian. Intellectual growth without spiritual growth is an unworthy goal for the Christian teacher.

The goal of knowledge and learning, like all other things, is to aid in loving God with the heart, soul, mind, and strength (Luke 10:27). As the mind is tuned and turned toward the truth, a right response to the God of truth is required. Engagement with the mind should lead to the bowing of the heart. Pearcey writes, "The renewal of our minds comes about only through the submission of our whole selves to the Lordship of Christ."[151] Every interaction, in and out of the classroom, is a chance to highlight the Lord and appeal to submission. This is discipleship. Therefore, Christian teachers are, by nature, engaged in the discipleship process.

Timothy Paul Jones defines discipleship as "a personal and intentional process in which one or more Christians guide

---

[149]Nancy Pearcey, *Total Truth: Liberating Christianity from Its Cultural Captivity* (Wheaton, IL: Crossway, 2005), 20.

[150]Ibid., 24.

[151]Ibid., 26.

unbelievers or less mature believers to embrace and apply the gospel in every part of their lives."[152] While this is the purpose of discipleship, there has been discussion in recent years concerning the target of discipleship. Should it be tilted toward the heart or mind? In his review of Christian philosopher James K. A. Smith's *Cultural Liturgy* series, David S. Morlan notes that Smith makes the case that "the center of gravity in the human person is much lower than the mind; it is in the bowels. . . . The individual is won or lost in the lower pre-cognitive emotional center of the person, and, more importantly, the world already knows this."[153]

However, Pearcey points out that many young people are turning from their faith because they have not been provided with the "intellectual resources" needed to interact with the ideologies challenging faith today.[154]

While there are differences in perspective, there is no need to create a false dichotomy between the two aims. Discipleship should target the head and heart to the mutual benefit

> **Quick Question**
> Does your teaching lean toward either the heart or mind?

of both. It is possible that the two are more connected than most realize and that those who are able to impact both are the most effective disciplers. C. S. Lewis is an example of one who married mind and heart as he "combined what almost everybody today assumes are mutually exclusive: rationalism and poetry, cool logic and warm feeling, disciplined prose and free imagination."[155] If Piper is a good example of the

[152]Timothy Paul Jones, *Family Ministry Field Guide: How Your Church Can Equip Parents to Make Disciples* (Indianapolis: Wesleyan Publishing House, 2011), 17.

[153]David S. Morlan, "A Review of James K. A. Smith's Cultural Liturgies Series," *Bulletin of Ecclesial Theology* 3, no. 1 (June 2016): 3.

[154]Pearcey, *Total Truth*, 32.

[155]Piper and Carson, *The Pastor as Scholar*, 34.

importance of integrated learning, Lewis is a picture of integrated teaching.

The Greatest Commandment is to love God fully and well (Matt 22:37-38). It is not a call to know much about Him. However, love and awe are deepened through knowing. Piper makes this argument:

> Right thinking about God exists to serve right feelings for God. Logic exists for the sake of love. Reasoning exists for the sake of rejoicing. Doctrine exists for the sake of delight. Reflection about God exists for the sake of affection for God. The head is meant to serve the heart.[156]

The Christian educator then is always aiming for the heart, but often through the avenue of the mind. There should be no battle between the two. Instead, the teacher's struggle is to wrestle with how to implement this integration clearly and consistently.

General and Special (The Content)

While engaging the heart and mind, the teacher is also highlighting connection between general and special revelation. In order to understand biblical integration, one must grasp what elements are being integrated, or united, together. The *how* is often dependent on the *what*. Two of the elements joined in biblical integration are general revelation and special revelation.

Charles Ryrie describes general revelation by saying that it "includes all that God has revealed in the world around

---

[156]Ibid., 50.

us, including man."[157] Therefore, every subject taught in school is an investigation into God's general revelation. Even though non-Christian instructors may not know it, all teachers are trying to help students understand what God has made. Science shines light on his world. Math highlights his order. History is his story. This world exists because God spoke it into being. The universe is his word in power. All that exists does so because He said so, which includes humanity itself.

What is man? Author and professor N. D. Wilson responds, "Words. Magic words. Words spoken by the Infinite, words so potent, spoken by One so potent that they have weight and mass and flavor. They are real. They have taken on flesh and dwelt among us. They are us."[158]

What is this world? Mankind and man's world are made of the same materials. Wilson continues, "We stand on a spoken stage. The spinning kind. The round kind. The moist kind. The kind of stage with beetles and laughter and babies and dirt and snow and fresh-cut cedar."[159] God breathed out the commands that made the world (Gen 1:3), the essence of life into Adam's nostrils (Gen 2:7), and the power for eternal life in his Scriptures (2 Tim 3:16). Therefore, Christians should see biblical integration as the uniting of the spoken world of God with the spoken Word of God. This unification is an important aspect of what makes Christian education Christian.

Zachary Eswine states, "As Creator/Redeemer, God preaches to us by verbal (special revelation) and non-verbal (general revelation) means."[160] Christian educators are tasked with bringing these elements together so that students see and hear God clearly. Pastors often lean into special revelation and

---

[157]Charles Caldwell Ryrie, *Basic Theology: A Popular Systematic Guide to Understanding Biblical Truth* (Chicago: Moody, 1999), 31.

[158]N. D. Wilson, *Notes from the Tilt-a-Whirl: Wide-Eyed Wonder in God's Spoken World* (Nashville: Thomas Nelson, 2009), loc. 382, Kindle.

[159]Ibid., loc. 387.

[160]Zachary W. Eswine, "Creation and Sermon: The Role of General Revelation in Biblical Preaching," *Presbyterion* 33, no. 1 (2007): 4

away from general revelation because it seems less innately theological.[161] Similarly, many educators lean away from Scripture because it can seem more devotional and less academic. However, if the goal of education is discipleship, both forms of God's communication must be investigated. Jared Longshore explains,

> God is the One who has written His law on the heart of humanity. He is the One who has created this world, ordered its events, and breathed out His holy Scriptures. Therefore, since the divine moral governor of the world has communicated to moral beings, those moral beings have an obligation, a duty, to attend to that revelation. Thus the very nature of revelation requires a spiritual life of study or heeding of the Word of God.[162]

This study of God's Word and world will, as Longshore notes, "Motivate joy and delight in the spiritual life."[163] Both general and special revelation contribute to the ability to find this joy in knowing God better. John Peter Lange explains that general revelation is "the foundation on which the special rests."[164] God spoke his Word into this world. Christ was born on earth. The Holy Spirit convicts and comforts people made of flesh and blood. The general is the atmosphere into which the Word is spoken. However, while the general is foundational, the special is needed. James Hoffmeier explains, "The revelation of God that is apprehended by looking at the expanse of the heavens, or any part of God's creation, is

---

[161]Ibid., 3.

[162]Jared R. Longshore, "Doctrine according to Godliness: The Spiritual Purpose of John L. Dagg's Manuel of Theology," *The Founders Journal* 96 (Spring 2014): 12.

[163]Ibid., 13.

[164]John Peter Lange et al., *Genesis: A Commentary on the Holy Scriptures* (Bellingham, WA: Logos Bible Software, 2008), 46-47.

limited to providing veiled information about God, but not what is necessary to know God in any intimate or salvine sense."[165]

General revelation communicates much about Him, but does not initiate relationship with God. Therefore, there is a need for the special. The conscience and the outside world can teach about God, but no other source can compare to God's Word.[166] It is clear and direct. It informs, instructs, and corrects in ways that general revelation is not able to do. The Christian educator brings together special and general revelation to develop knowledge of God that leads to joy in a deeper relationship with Him. This is an essential element of biblical integration. It is what makes biblical integration truly biblical.

Word and Deed (The Means)

Teachers target the heart through the mind and reunite the spoken world and holy Word by the means of words as well as deeds. These two avenues of instruction could be called, as noted by Elizabeth Sites, "The Infusion of Faith in Pedagogy and The Demonstration of Faith in Relationships."[167] In other words, the Christian educator speaks and models the unity of faith with scholarship — teachers must show and tell.

> **Nerd Note**
> *Pedagogy* refers to the way teaching is practiced — especially the theory or reason behind the way one does it.

---

[165]James K. Hoffmeier, "'The Heavens Declare the Glory of God': The Limits of General Revelation," *Trinity Journal* 21, no.1 (Spring 2000): 20.

[166]Longshore, "Doctrine according to Godliness," 12.

[167]Elizabeth C. Sites, et al., "A Phenomenology of the Integration of Faith and Learning," *Journal of Psychology & Theology* 37, no. 1 (2009): 33.

The dual method of word and deed demonstrates the presence and power of God in a way that delivers a robust vision of the good life. Classroom lessons alone are not enough. Morlan makes the case that "cultural forces . . . function as a sort of liturgy and direct what we actually worship. The world offers embodied practices that shape our desires and provide a compelling vision of what the good life is."[168] It is the task of the teacher to do more than pass on knowledge, but to invite students into a cultural liturgy of truth through relationship.

The world appeals to students through experience—the lust of the flesh, the lust of the eyes, and the pride of life (1 John 2:16). It calls them to engage in actions, thoughts, and attitudes that promise satisfaction. This experience is illustrated by the parable of the Lost Son in Luke 15. The son leaves what he knows to be true and right in search of experiencing what he expects will be more satisfying. When the world left him bankrupt and starving, he came to his senses and turned for home. Morlan identifies the son's experience as his pivotal moment: "That was the transition that led to repentance and reconciliation."[169] He had done more than hear his father's words throughout his life, but had experienced a relationship with him.

Robert Webber sums up his experience with instruction that comes from word divorced from deed when he writes, "Christianity was no longer a power to be experienced but a system to be defended."[170] He understood that Christianity is about more than a system of thinking, but a God to be known. Discipleship is something learned through more than just words, but through practice. Matthew Ward points to "practices that are caught, not taught, practices that must be repeated until habitualized, practices that demonstrate the

---

[168]Morlan, "A Review of James K. A. Smith's Cultural Liturgies Series," 3.

[169]Morlan, "A Review of James K. A. Smith's Cultural Liturgies Series," 10.

[170]Matthew Ward, "Kingdom Worship: James K. A. Smith, Robert Webber and Western Civilization," *Bulletin of Ecclesial Theology* 3, no. 1 (June 2016): 130.

church as a counter-culture."[171] These practices are transmitted through people. They are to be passed from teacher to student.

It is at the intersection of truth and action that word meets deed. In relationship with the students, teachers are to model true Christlikeness and engage the students in that lifestyle. Kenneth Badley confirms, "The character and attitudes of teachers and professors offer another obvious venue for faith-learning integration."[172] Students must see the truth and value of Christianity in the lives of their instructors. Without works, they will have reason to believe that faith is dead (Jas 2). The life of the teacher is to illustrate and complement the lessons taught in the classroom. In this way, the students will not only know the *what* and *why* of Christianity, but also the *how*.

Conclusion

John Piper writes, "The mind is supposed to be engaged in seeing reality for what it is, and awakening the heart to love God for all that he is."[173] The goal of biblical integration is to engage students in seeing things the way they really are. By reuniting heart with mind, general with special revelation, and word with deed, instructors will be able to successfully disciple students. They will share in Piper's goal as they help their pupils to:

> think rightly and deeply about the Word and the world with a view to seeing the greatness of God and his works (especially the work of Christ) so that the affections of our hearts might rest on a true foundation

[171]Ibid., 132.
[172]Badley, "Clarifying 'Faith-Learning Integration,'" 8.
[173]Piper and Carson, *The Pastor as Scholar*, 52.

and God might be honored by how we feel toward him and by the behaviors that flow from this heart.[174]

Speaking to teachers, Hendricks makes the case for the arduous work of truly Christian education: "God wants to use you as his catalyst—and as you let him transform and renew your thinking, you'll be ready for his use."[175] God can do mighty things through the teacher who will yield the classroom to Him. However, this task is not easy. Hendricks continues with the challenge, "Are we willing to pay the price for development? There is, after all, a cost involved. Effective teaching isn't available at any bargain basement sale."[176] Reuniting what the world and the field of education has long divided is a challenge. The work is hard and the cost is high. However, the reward is worth it as teachers train their pupils to pursue a life where they request in harmony with David, "May these words of my mouth and this meditation of my heart be pleasing in your sight, LORD, my Rock and my Redeemer" (Ps 19:14).

---

[174]Ibid.

[175]Hendricks, *Teaching to Change Lives*, 130.

[176]Ibid.

Part Three

Curriculum Articles

The following articles were created to be used as a component of the *Every Bush is Burning* training. After building a foundation for biblical integration in Parts 1 & 2, this section of the book is intended to help educators put their understanding into practice.

Teachers will learn to grow into incarnational, intentional instigators—leaders who demonstrate the reality of the Christian faith through their lives, and help their students grow in worldview thinking.

The *Every Bush is Burning* training will help teachers learn how to model, plan, and carry out biblical integration in their classrooms.

Instructions

If you are using this book as a part of the *Every Bush is Burning* interactive training, **stop** reading here. But you should have the book handy when attending the training. You will need it.

If you are using this book apart from the formal training event, read on.

01: Starting with Honesty

There are few knives that cut a Christian educator like seeing students turn from the Christian faith after graduating. It is painful and worrisome. Why does this kind of transition seem so common? Nancy Pearcey relays a story about a young man who "lost [his] faith at an evangelical college."[177] This student wanted to know how the Christian faith was related to the academic content taught in the college classroom. However, the instructors taught their material just like any secular school would. Math was just math. History was only history. Instructors did not offer a robust biblical worldview in these classes. Pearcey says that this story "reflects an all-too-common pattern today."[178]

While Christian teachers often believe what C.S. Lewis articulated by saying, "Every bush (could we but perceive it) is a Burning Bush,"[179] without biblical integration, students are not equipped to see and understand God's glory and purpose for his world. How many students are rejecting the Person and plan of Christ because we are not effectively practicing biblical integration? Many. And I am confident that the number is much higher than just those who have turned fully or thoughtfully from the faith. Many are not rejecting as much as they are disconnecting. And this is equally tragic. Drift can also lead to drowning.

Pearcey tells of another individual who had not engaged thoughtfully with worldview questions. Instead, she had isolated in order to keep herself safe. She did not study and weigh other truth claims and ways of life. Therefore, Pearcey shares, "Because she had never studied their ideas, she had no grid to recognize and reject them."[180] Her lack of

---

[177]Nancy Pearcey, *Finding Truth: 5 Principles for Unmasking Atheism, Secularism, and Other God Substitutes* (Colorado Springs: David C. Cook, 2015), 21.

[178]Ibid., 22.

[179]C. S. Lewis, *Letters to Malcolm: Chiefly on Prayer*, (Orlando: Harcourt, 1963), 75.

[180]Pearcey, *Finding Truth*, 53.

interaction and understanding had allowed her to unknowingly inject non-Christian ideas and values into her life. She was turning away without even knowing it.

Craig Groeschel wrote a book entitled, *The Christian Atheist: Believing in God but Living as If He Doesn't Exist*. The subtitle offers the definition of a term that is embodied in many Christian schools. Christian Atheism can be rightly seen as the direct opposite of biblical integration. It is compartmentalized thinking that leads to compartmentalized living. The question needs to be asked, "Are students embracing Christian Atheism because of the outside culture, or are they being taught this way in our schools?"

We need to begin with an honest assessment of our practices. Could it be that our lack of integration leads to rejection and disconnection? Are we "protecting" our students now at the cost of their futures? Are our classrooms the natural habitat of Christian atheists?

Discussion Questions

What do you think motivates young people to reject Christianity today?

What is the difference between rejection and disconnection?

What dangers might be associated with isolating and protecting students from other worldviews?

Where do you notice Christian Atheism practiced in teaching and learning?

02: A Vision of Success

My goal is to equip you to be incarnational, intentional instigators so that you can come close to your students with a plan to break the spell of compartmentalized living and thinking. John Frame defines *theology* as "the application of the Word of God, by persons, to every area of life."[181] Christian teachers must be theologians in the sense that we are applying God's Word to our academic areas. And we must help our students to become theologians as well. The teacher who embraces Frame's definition of theology will embrace biblical integration.

Biblical integration is teaching students to reconcile God's Word and world by recognizing that all things are from and for Him. In order to teach in this fashion, instructors must be incarnational (representing Christ to students), intentional (thoughtfully planning course material for students), and instigating (creating healthy conflict between the Christian and non-Christian worldviews). Successful integrators are incarnational, intentional instigators. We are to set the example by modeling an integrated life, set the table by designing courses for purposeful worldview engagement, and set the fight by showing the incompatibility of certain presuppositions and conclusions.

This kind of teaching will affect the students and, through their lives, the culture at large. The King's College in New York City makes their priorities for cultural impact clear in their mission statement which says:

> Through its commitment to the truths of Christianity and a biblical worldview, The King's College seeks to transform society by preparing students for careers in which they help to shape and eventually to lead

---

[181]John Frame, *John Frame's Selected Shorter Writings* (Phillipsburg, NJ: P & R, 2015), 2:61.

strategic public and private institutions, and by supporting faculty members as they directly engage culture through writing and speaking publicly on critical issues.[182]

Likewise, the Christian Thinkers Society exists, according to their mission statement, "to reach a new demographic and demonstrate why Christianity makes sense, is enriching to life, and why it is essential for the betterment of society."[183] Like the Christian Thinkers Society, Christian teachers are striving to show God and his ways as true, good, and beautiful. How is this accomplished in the classroom setting? Through incarnational, intentional instigating.

Christian educators are interested in much more than passing on knowledge. What does a student gain if he gets all the knowledge in the world but loses his soul? (Mark 8:36). To teach any content apart from its worldview implications is to choose to leave God out of that area. Can we be comfortable with picking and choosing where to insert God into his own kingdom and creation? Of course not. If you are a Christian educator, you are a theologian. That means applying the Word to your area in example, academic direction, and discussion.

---

[182]The Kings' College, "About King's," accessed May 12, 2017, https://www.tkc.edu/about-kings/.

[183]Christian Thinkers, accessed May 12, 2017, http://christianthinkers.com/.

Discussion Questions

What do you think it looks like to apply God's Word to your area/subject?

Where are you naturally strong or weak in the school setting — Modeling the faith incarnationally? Planning integration intentionally? Instigating worldview conflict regularly?

Are you committed to biblical integration as your highest purpose as a teacher? What are the obstacles to doing so?

Training 1

The Incarnational Teacher

Become a teacher who embodies Christ by taking the form of a servant. Learn to show love to students by knowing them and showing them the Good News. This type of worldview living is a foundational component of effective worldview teaching. Biblical integration starts with Christ-like love.

03: Understanding Incarnation

The Oxford Dictionary of the Church describes the incarnation of Christ by saying, "The eternal Son of God took flesh from His human mother... the historical Christ is at once both fully God and fully man."[184] In Christ, God entered into humanity and disclosed his identity in a personal and hands-on fashion. Mankind was able to see God in close proximity.

Incarnational teachers seek to demonstrate the character of God through actions and attitudes, in addition to words. Just as God showed Himself through the work of Christ, incarnational teachers seek to allow Him to show Himself through the working of the Holy Spirit. God came into our world, and, as incarnational teachers, we enter the world of the students.

The word "incarnation" literally means "enfleshment" or "embodiment."[185] The idea is God with skin on. The body of Christ is now in a position to live into the mission of God by embodying the Good News. Charles Ryrie explained the incarnational model of ministry,

> Just as God performed His great work in the world through the incarnation of Christ, so now He continues that work through Christians in whom Christ is continually incarnated. Just as God was in Christ coming to the rescue of the world, so now Christ is in believers to continue His work.[186]

[184]F. L. Cross and Elizabeth A. Livingstone, eds., *The Oxford Dictionary of the Christian Church* (Oxford; New York: Oxford University Press, 2005), 830.

[185]C. Stephen Evans, *Pocket Dictionary of Apologetics & Philosophy of Religion* (Downers Grove, IL: InterVarsity, 2002), 59.

[186]Charles C. Ryrie, *Dr. Ryrie's Articles* (Bellingham, WA: Logos Bible Software, 2010), 120.

How do we continue in his work? Jesus came to serve rather than to be served (Mark 10:45). This means that if we are to represent Christ to students, we must follow his example by being their servants. Paul was clear that those who give themselves for others in costly service are following the example of Christ.[187] But what does it look like to serve in the school setting?

According to David Wheeler, those who are able to share Christ *informationally* and live those biblical truths *incarnationally* are able to demonstrate a compelling and holistic gospel.[188] Jesus said that his followers would be recognized by how they love (John 13:35). Peter ties words and deeds together saying,

> Always be prepared to give an answer to everyone who asks you to give the reason for the hope that you have. But do this with gentleness and respect, keeping a clear conscience, so that those who speak maliciously against your good behavior in Christ may be ashamed of their slander. (1 Pet 3:15b-16)

Teachers must not only be ready to share the reasons for their faith, they must also demonstrate its reality through gentleness and respect. The presentation of information through incarnation paints such a clear picture of the living God that those who speak against believers are ashamed. John gives the reason for this, saying, "No one has ever seen God. But if we love each other, God lives in us, and his love is brought to full expression in us" (1 John 4:12).

---

[187]Ibid., 121.

[188]David Wheeler, "Incarnational Apologetics," in *The Popular Encyclopedia of Apologetics*, ed. Ed Hindson and Ergun Caner (Eugene, OR: Harvest House, 2008), 51.

When Christians live their faith by loving, God is clearly seen for who He really is. His love is fully expressed. And we long to see Him fully expressed in the classroom.

Every day, students should encounter the full expression of God's love. Those who do not yet know the Lord should experience truth married to such gentleness and respect that their Christ-less worldview is put to shame. This is how we hope to serve them. We must strive to be the complete picture of God's love with skin on.

Discussion Questions

Do your students see you as their servant? Why or why not?

Does your service to students demonstrate that God has radically changed your life? Is it evidence of the reality of the Good News?

Do your interactions with students demonstrate the full expression of God's love?

04: Reenacting the Gospel

Paul and Timothy loved the disciples in Thessalonica so much that they "were delighted to share... not only the gospel of God but [their] lives as well" (1 Thess 2:8). They gave much more than information. They gave themselves. They showed the gospel through their lives. Trevin Wax points to the importance of the teacher as an interactive model to students by explaining,

> Disciple-making is accomplished by modelers, not just messengers. We develop not merely through cognitive transfer, but also through witnessing the lives and choices of other disciples we encounter on our way... The teachers who make the biggest difference on our lives are those who not only give us knowledge but who know us well enough to speak truth into the specifics of our lives, to give counsel from their vast experience and biblical storehouse.[189]

Modeling, by all teachers and staff, is necessary because students see as well as hear. If a Christian school emphasizes loving others in Bible classes, but winning and achieving at all costs in sports and academics, there will be a disconnect.[190] The students need to see and recognize the Good News in our lives as they hear and interact with it in their own.

---

[189]Trevin Wax, "The Revenge of Analog Discipleship," accessed May 13, 2017, http://blogs.thegospelcoalition.org/trevinwax/2017/05/11/the-revenge-of-analog-discipleship/.

[190]Gloria Goris Stronks and Doug Blomberg, eds., "A Vision with a Task: Christian School for Responsive Discipleship," 28, accessed May 13, 2017, http://www.calvin.edu/academic/education/news/publications/monoweb/vision/pdf.htm.

Jesus stated that the greatest love is laying down one's life for a friend (John 15:13). Therefore, we should show our students love by laying down our lives for them. In Philippians 2, Paul points to Jesus as our example of how to do this:

1) He didn't cling to his status. He didn't allow his God-ness to keep Him from us. Instead, He used his high stature to lift us up.
2) He entered our world. Jesus didn't speak to us from afar. Instead, He stooped down and squeezed his God-ness into a human form.
3) He humbled Himself to the position of a servant. As mentioned previously, the One who has every right to be served chose to be our servant.
4) He gave up his life. There was no limit to his willingness to serve. There was no gift too big or sacrifice too costly.

What was the result of the Messiah's incarnational love? God was glorified. Everything that Jesus did was "to the glory of the Father" (Phil 2:11). The glory of God is the definition of success. If God is glorified in your class, you are doing what you were called to do.

How do we glorify the Father like Christ did? By giving up status, entering our students' world, becoming their servants, and laying down our lives for them. We are to reenact the gospel before their eyes and in their lives.

Discussion Questions

What does it look like to share our lives with our students? Are you doing that?

In what ways do you enter your students' world instead of loving them from your own?

Do you see yourself as a servant to your students? What are the primary ways in which you serve them?

Practical Tip: Choose Some to Love All

In *The Lost Art of Disciple Making,* LeRoy Eims said, "Whoever is thinking about or is now involved in a ministry of making disciples (Matt. 28:19) should think soberly about… selection."[191] It is not possible to be close with a hundred students. Jesus was compassionate to the masses and taught the crowd, but He was friends with Lazarus, Martha, and Mary. And He discipled just twelve men. However, his method changed the world.

Eims continued, "He had two things in mind in the training of the Twelve. One, that they would be of help to Him then and there in carrying out His mission. Two, that they would carry on after He was gone."[192] These are two things to keep in mind as you teach. Who can you pour into so that they will assist your work and so that they will carry it on after your class is over?

Who can you select to intentionally disciple this year? How can you go about investing in them?

[191]LeRoy Eims, *The Lost Art of Disciple Making* (Grand Rapids: Zondervan, 1978), 29.

[192]Ibid., 34.

Training 2

The Intentional Teacher

*Learn to intentionally plan your courses
and units from and toward the glory and
reality of God. Grow in your ability to
design and assess biblically integrated
courses and rightly handle Scripture. This is
hands-on help in doing efficient, effective, and
faithful integration.*

05: The Bible and Biblical Integration

Since teachers have a pastoral role, we must know how to handle the Bible. In Isaiah 66:2, God says that He is pleased with those who are humble and tremble before his Word. In Hebrews 4:12, God's Word is described as sharper than a two-edged sword. It pierces and penetrates to the deepest parts. Teachers must employ Scripture in biblical integration. To do otherwise is like performing surgery without a scalpel. The Word of God is the only way to make the needed cut. However, because of its great power, it must be used properly.

Why has God given teachers such a sharp sword? Again, Hebrews 4:12 explains that it is to judge thoughts and attitudes of the heart. But the Word does more than cut — it heals and saves. The disciples recognized this in John 6:68, saying to Jesus, "Lord, to whom should we go? You have the words that give eternal life." In light of the slicing and saving power of the words of God, John Piper challenges:

> Give yourself to this word so that your words become the word of God for others and reveal to them their own spiritual condition. Then in the wound of the word, pour the balm of the word.[193]

This is the task of the integrating teacher. There is no use in looking to transform lives by any other means. Albert Mohler contends, "The Word will have to do the work, or the work will not be done."[194] Just as the words of God brought life and form to the universe, so Scripture transforms the world today. Therefore, teachers must have a strong

[193] John Piper, "Pierced by the Word of God," October 3, 2001, accessed May 13, 2017, http://www.desiringgod.org/articles/pierced-by-the-word-of-god.

[194] R. Albert Mohler, quoted in S. Craig Sanders, "From the Seminaries: Mohler on the Reformation at SBTS Convocation; Midwestern Launches in-the-field M.Div," *Baptist Press*, February 15, 2017, accessed May 13, 2017, http://www.bpnews.net/48340.

commitment to the Word and a powerful ability to properly employ it.

In 2 Timothy 2:14-16, Paul connects the workman approved by God to the one who handles the Word of truth correctly. He also contrasts those who employ the Word with those who engage in godless chatter. A lesson that is uninformed by the Word of God, even in the confines of a Christian school or church, is godless chatter. In the same way, teachings that use Scripture out of context or incorrectly, are godless as well. There can be no biblical integration without the proper use of the Bible itself.

Discussion Questions

What does "The Word will have to do the work," mean in practice?

How and when do you use the Bible in your class? In planning? In prayer? As the basis for discussion? Other?

What kind of reaction does "godless chatter" cause in you? Is unintegrated teaching really godless chatter?

06: How to Handle Our Weapon – What Not to Do

Many Christians, even those who have been reading the Bible for a long time, struggle to understand it correctly. There are many bad habits and misconceptions built into church culture that lead committed readers off track. For example, perhaps you can recall someone in a Bible study saying something along the lines of, "To me, this passage means…" or "God spoke to me through this passage by saying…" While it is important to look for meaning and to hear God's voice, we need to make sure that we are not trying to put our words into his mouth. He can speak for Himself. Andy Naselli explains, "When people interpret the Bible, even though they may have the best motives in the world, they can still read their ideas into the Bible rather than draw out what the author originally intended."[195]

Our culture celebrates individualism and employs postmodernism. These forces lead Christians to think that the Bible can mean something "to me" that it doesn't mean to others. However, this is not the case.

When we read, we should want to find the one true meaning of the text. And there is only one. That meaning is the message that the author was trying to convey in the first place. We are not trying to find a special message that specifically applies to us or our circumstances (that mistake is called "personalizing,") or discover an ethical lesson in every passage (that mistake is called "moralizing.") Here is an example of how we might go wrong in these ways.

Personalizing and moralizing are both found in how some people commonly interpret Matthew 14:22-33. Perhaps you have heard someone read the story of Jesus and Peter walking on water and equate the boat to a "comfort zone," or made the message about "keeping your eyes on Jesus." They

---

[195]Andrew David Naselli, *How to Understand and Apply the New Testament: Twelve Steps from Exegesis to Theology* (Phillipsburg, NJ: P & R, 2017), 3.

might say that Jesus calling Peter out of the boat is an example of how He calls us out on the "water" in our lives, or that we need to keep our eyes on Him through the storms of life. The idea is that this story is an allegory of us and our circumstances. However, this is not an accurate reading. How do we know that?

First, we see that we are not meant to imitate Peter here. The passage is descriptive rather than prescriptive. Upon seeing Jesus on the water, the disciples cried out in fear. Jesus responded by reassuring them. However, Peter did not take Him at his word, but tested Him. Instead of listening to Christ, Peter then told Jesus what to do. Jesus gracefully agreed, but the reason that Jesus called Peter out of the boat was because Peter instructed Him to do so. And, once on the water, the reason Peter began to doubt was because of fear of wind and wave. It was likely not because he looked away from Christ since the passage does not even speak to that. As Peter sank, he cried out for help and Jesus rescued him.

Second, this passage is not about comfort zones or keeping our eyes on Jesus, but about the awesome power and kindness of Christ. He can walk on water. He can cause others to do that too. He can save those who are sinking. And in the end, the disciples worship Him and declare that He is the Son of God. If we are distracted into the personalized message that we should get out of our comfort zone or the moralized message of ignoring the storm to look to Him, we will miss the real message of the passage—Jesus is the Son of God and He is worthy of worship.

So what are we meant to look for as we read? Gordan Fee and Douglas Stuart explain, "The aim of a good interpretation is simple: to get at the 'plain meaning of the text,' the author's intended meaning."[196] This aim will help us to read the Bible to discover the meaning that the Holy Spirit

---

[196]Gordon D. Fee and Douglas Stuart, *How to Read the Bible for All Its Worth,* 4th ed. (Grand Rapids: Zondervan, 2014), 22.

inspired the author to communicate. And isn't that better than any other message we could hope to receive?

Discussion Questions

Why is the temptation to moralize and personalize our readings so strong? What causes us to read Scripture this (incorrect) way?

What is the difference between a prescriptive and a descriptive passage in the Bible?

07: How to Handle Our Weapon – What to Do

How do we get to the author's intended meaning when we read the Bible? I suggest we start with common sense to carefully look for context, characters, and consistency.

Careful Reading

Hearing what the author said in his time and context is called "exegesis," and Andy Naselli says, "Exegesis is simply careful reading."[197] Many mistakes come from rushed or careless reading. Many misinterpretations could be avoided if we slowed down to notice the text and to notice our biases. Fee and Stuart tell us that the key exegesis "to learn to read the text carefully and to ask the right questions of the text."[198]

Context

The first question to ask is about context. Fee and Stuart share the key truth that, "A text cannot mean what it could never have meant for its original readers/hearers."[199] We need to try to understand Isaiah the way the people in his day would have. We need to try to grasp Mark's telling of the Good News in the way that his original audience would have.

For example, in Philippians 4:13, Paul said, "I can do all things through him who gives me strength." What would the Philippian church have heard him saying? Would they have heard him say, "I can do anything—like breathe underwater—though him who gives me strength."? No. The verses leading up this show us the context. There Paul is talking about his ability to be content in any situation. Therefore, we see that

---

[197]Naselli, *How to Understand and Apply the New Testament*, 1

[198]Fee and Stuart, *How to Read the Bible*, 30.

[199]Ibid., 34.

Paul is saying that he can be content, through the power of Christ, in any situation.

Characters

Our next key task is to remember that, while the whole Bible is for us, it was not originally written to us. Therefore, we need to understand who the characters are in the text. We need to know who is speaking and who is being spoken to. For example, in 2 Timothy 4:13, Paul gives the command to bring him his cloak. Thankfully, we know he isn't talking to us, so we don't have to invest in a trip to Troas to find his clothes. That is an obvious and silly example, but there are times when we mess this up. Think about Jeremiah 29:11. In this passage, God tells about the good and prosperous plans he has for "you." But who is the "you" in Jeremiah 29:11? Certainly, this was not addressed to all the high school graduates that receive mugs with this verse printed on it. God is talking to an ancient people that is entering exile. He is telling them to invest in their exilic community. He wants them to build homes and families there. And after a time, he will bring them back to Israel.

In the classroom, it is up to the teacher to show the students what faithful reading looks like. The Bible does teach that God is good and has wonderful plans for us as his people. However, we must be careful not to stretch verses by making them about us when the Holy Spirit intended them to be about others. While the instructor may rightly understand the wide biblical truth that God does have good plans for us as his people, we need to intentionally model correct patterns of study for students who may soak up what we intentionally and unintentionally teach.

Consistency

Finally, read the Bible with the rest of the Bible as your commentary. God does not change. He does not contradict Himself. This helps us understand what we are reading. For instance, when Ecclesiastes says that everything is meaningless, should we believe that? Well, the Bible does say that. But we know from God's consistent character and message that life matters. Life can *feel* meaningless at times. And the one who lives without God is truly living a meaningless life.

Not everything in the Bible is prescribed. Thankfully, much is only described. In addition, not everything in the Bible is universal. Jesus does not call everyone to bathe in order to be healed. He does not want mud applied to every blind eye. It is important that we read the Bible with the rest of it in mind. This will help us stay on track.

Practical Help

I propose reading in three steps — information, understanding, and action.[200]

Information: What does this passage say? Sum it up in your own words.

Understanding: What does it mean? Why does it matter? What does it say about God? What universal principles can be found here?

Action: What should I think, do, or be in response?

---

[200]Mark Strauss recommends these four questions: (1) Where is this passage in the larger story of Scripture? (2) What is the author's purpose in light of the passage's genre and historical and literary context? (3) How does this passage inform our understanding of the nature of God and his purpose for the world? (4) What does this passage teach us about who we ought to be (attitudes and character) and what we ought to do (goals and actions) as those seeking to reflect the nature and purpose of God? Mark L. Strauss, *How to Read the Bible in Changing Times: Understanding and Applying God's Word Today* (Grand Rapids: Baker, 2011), 78-79, Kindle.

08: Integration Helps Teacher and Student

While some instructors struggle with the idea of integration because they worry about the time or focus it will take from their instruction, if done with intentionality, Bradley McCoy, a physics professor at Azusa Pacific University, found that "no reduction of… content at all was necessary in order to implement the faith integration curriculum."[201] Indeed, it is possible that the students could be more engaged and invested in course content because they clearly see the application of the course content in their lives.

We have all heard the dreaded question from our students, "Why do I need to learn this? Why is it important?" They want to know why ancient history or the parts of a flower should matter to them. Biblical integration answers that question in the most satisfying way possible. It does not sidestep the students' true core question of "What's in this for me?" by pointing to Christ. Biblical integration points to God as the ultimate reward and satisfaction. This allows for a deep connection between the student and the subject. It also engenders partnership between the students and the teacher because they are on a quest together. They are seeking the glorious unifying factor in all things—the Lord Himself.

In addition, teachers can remain enthusiastic about the often-difficult task of teaching when they understand that they are disciple-makers. Instructors can get frustrated when the job is understood as piles of grading, daily discipline struggles, and hectic schedules. Integration allows the teacher to access the deeper purpose to which they were called.

However, even if academic content must be sacrificed from time to time, teachers must remain committed to their first calling—distinctively Christian education. Can excellent non-Christian education be considered a success for followers

---

[201]Bradley K. McCoy, "Developing a Program-Level Faith Integration Curriculum: A Case Study from Physics," *Christian Higher Education* 13 (December 2014): 348

of Jesus? Not in the Christian school context. We must never sacrifice the Eternal for the passing or the Author for the book.

But while integration is necessary, it is not easy. The curator of BiblicalIntegration.com points out some of the main reasons that teachers may not want to write biblically integrated lesson plans:

- It takes too long.
- They don't know what to integrate.
- It's too hard (there's no easy format).
- It's one more thing to do, it's an add-on.[202]

If integration is a time-consuming, confusing, difficult add-on, it can be very frustrating. Teachers are busy and don't have time for extra assignments. The goal here is to help you create quality biblical integration that is time-friendly, clear, and central to your class.

> **Discussion Questions**
>
> Do you view biblical integration as a struggle or a privilege? Is it an add-on or is it a driving force in your teaching?
>
> What are the greatest barriers to your ability to practice excellent biblical integration?

---

[202]Biblical Integration, "Lesson Plan Worksheet," accessed May 19, 2017, http://biblicalintegration.com/write-a-lesson-plan/.

09: Purposeful Course Design

James Estep says that curriculum is the "educational manifestation of the mission and vision" of a teaching organization.[203] What we plan to teach shows us what we care about. This means that we can look at our syllabi to see what drives us. At the start of the year, the syllabus is like a treasure map — it plots the course to success. The problem is that many Christian teachers are not plotting a course that aligns with what Christian schools see as true success. The curriculum, Estep continues, is a "tangible representation and incarnation of our educational philosophy."[204] Do our syllabi align with our educational philosophy? To find out, we must look at our syllabus to find the null curriculum, the foundation, and the aim.

Null Curriculum

The biggest decision that a teacher makes when developing a course is what not to teach. There is far too much in any subject to be covered even in a multi-year sequence at the secondary school level. Null curriculum is what the teacher has chosen to leave out and this is always the majority of information.[205] So what gets left out? And how do we decide what will not be included?

Foundation

No course exists in a vacuum. Every presupposition in the syllabus is built on something. Teachers must identify the foundation of the course in order to determine how to teach it

---

[203]James Estep, *Mapping Out Curriculum in Your Church* (Nashville: B & H, 2012), locs. 124-26, Kindle.

[204]Ibid., locs. 250-52.

[205]Ibid., locs. 279-81.

well. What ideas, assumptions, truths, theories, ideologies, or other factors determine the make-up of this class? As a Bible teacher, my courses are undeniably shaped by the fact that I believe that there is a God, and that He has spoken. In the same way, every history course is shaped by views on God's work throughout time. Every science class is built on ideas and understandings. We often take these for granted, but that is a mistake.

Aim

Finally, the direction that the course is pointing must be considered. What does it equip the students to know or do? And why does it point them that way? In other words, we need to know the purpose of our classes.

Discussion Activity: Examining a Syllabus

The following is the course description from a high school speech class at my school. Jeffrey Prussia is the (legendary) teacher of this class and he has graciously allowed us access to his syllabus for use in this work.

Speech is a course designed to teach students effective Speech Communication. Students will study responsible and ethical communication. Students will learn how to articulate through delivering different types of speeches such as persuasive, demonstration, informative, oratory speeches, interviews and how to debate in parliamentary procedure.[206]

Identify the foundation and aim of this course. What is it built on? Why does it aim toward?

---

[206]Jeff Prussia, "High School Speech (syllabus, The King's Academy, 2016-2017).

Now read the altered course description below. Identify the foundation and aim of this course. What is it built on? Why does it aim toward?

Speech is a course designed to teach students effective Speech Communication. Since speech is a powerful gift that reflects God's glory (Gen 1:3), a potentially dangerous weapon (Jas 3:5-6), a means through which we know the Lord (Gen 2:16-17), and an avenue for praise (Psalm 19:14), students will study responsible and ethical communication. Since the Good News is a message that must be shared (Rom 10:14) with people who see it as foolishness (1 Cor 1:18), students will learn how to articulate through delivering different types of speeches such as persuasive (Acts 17:17), demonstration, informative (1 Cor 12), oratory speeches (Matt 5), interviews (Luke 1:1-4) and how to debate in parliamentary procedure.

What can we expect to be different about these two courses?

What is different concerning the two courses' null curriculum?

Is it ever appropriate for biblical integration to be a part of the null curriculum?

10: It's Not an Add-On When It's in the DNA

Starting with an integrated syllabus is key to executing an integrated course. When you start by making biblical integration part of the ingrained identity of the class, it will naturally appear throughout. When a student looks at the syllabus, they may ask themselves, "What is this class all about?" You and your students can be on the same page with a well-developed syllabus. And as you can see from the previous example, you don't need to discard your old syllabi to practice integration. Instead, you can thoughtfully adapt them to make them what they are meant to be.

Once the syllabus has removed biblical integration from the null curriculum and placed it front-and-center, you can start to wrestle with the foundations and aims of the course more fully. This means asking questions. For the course description of our speech class, we might ask questions like:

- Where did speech come from? Why did God give it? What is its purpose?
- What dangers are associated with speech? Why must speech be ethical and responsible?
- What role does speech play in relationship? How does God speak to us? Why did God entrust us with the spoken message of Good News?

Instead of writing lesson plans and then integrating them after they are made, teachers should have the course's essential questions in mind when they develop the course. Gloria Goris Stronks and Doug Blomberg explain, "An integrally Christian curriculum cannot be developed by adding a spiritual veneer to so-called factual subject matter. The curriculum must find its coherence throughout as responsiveness to God speaking to us in Christ, creation, and

Scripture...*[207] The biblical integration, especially the core group of questions, is the design of the class.

So once the teacher designs the syllabus and identifies some key questions, the next step is mapping, or unit-planning, with those questions in mind. Mapping out instruction for a semester or year is a widely-accepted best-practice for staying on target and on time.[208] Major questions might be recurring or they may be associated with certain units during the year. When we are aware of the questions and when they should be brought up, we can create structured and unstructured time for engagement. It is a good idea for all instructors to build opportunities for students to think deeply about these questions, wrestle with ideas, and be creative in their responses. These moments can be some of the most rewarding for teachers.[209] And they are some of the most important for students.

Worldview expert Jeremiah Johnston emphasizes the importance of working through life's big questions, saying, "After ten years of serving as the teaching pastor of a mega church, I noticed we had sincere Christians attending church services weekly, listening to sermon after sermon, and yet they still did not possess the confidence to answer the tough questions being asked about Christianity."[210] Questions are key in Christian education.

When the syllabus is designed with integration in mind, and when the major questions are foundationally included in each unit of the course, there is very little work involved in writing individually integrated lessons. Integration is already in the course's DNA.

---

[207]Stronks and Blomberg, "A Vision with a Task," 109.

[208]Cindi Banse, "Purposeful Success for the School Year," *Math by Design* 9 no. 1 (August 2013): n.p.

[209]James Schwartz, "Rise to the Challenge," *Math by Design* 10 no. 2 (January 2015): n.p.

[210]Christian Thinkers, "The Unanswered Tour," accessed May 12, 2017, http://christianthinkers.com/unanswered/.

Discussion Activity: Lesson Planning

The textbook for our speech class is *Speech: Communication Matters* by McCutcheon, Schaffer, and Wycoff. The first chapter includes the following learning objectives:[211]

1. Identify and analyze the ethical and social responsibilities of communicators.

2. Identify the components of the communication process and their functions.

3. Explain the importance of effective communication skills in personal, professional, and social contexts.

4. Recognize your audience as an important element in building responsible communication skills.

5. Realize the importance and impact of both verbal and nonverbal communication.

Earlier, we noted that we might ask the questions, "Where did speech come from? Why did God give it? What is its purpose?" in our course. This set of questions can help us easily identify some great content to wrestle with in our first chapter. In fact, we don't even have to change the lesson objectives to make this chapter fully integrated. When we "identify and analyze the ethical and social responsibilities of communicators," (Objective 1) we will see that:

[211]Randall McCutcheon, James Schaffer, and Joseph Wycoff, *Speech: Communication Matters* (Chicago: National Textbook Company, 2001), 3.

- we are responsible to God concerning our communication because He gave it to us,

- God gave the ethical and social responsibility to represent Him well through speech

- the purpose of speech is, in large part, relationship and truth.

We can take those concepts as far as we deem appropriate in each class.

Our task is to identify how our over-arching integration questions (below) can be used in conjunction with Objectives 2-5 (above) from Chapter One of our speech textbook.

Where did speech come from? Why did God give it? What is its purpose?

What dangers are associated with speech? Why must speech be ethical and responsible?

What role does speech play in relationship? How does God speak to us? Why did God entrust us with the spoken message of Good News?

NOTE: This strategy not only works with chapter/unit objectives, but also with vocabulary and concepts. The first chapter of *Speech: Communication Matters* has a vocabulary list that includes these terms: *Ethics, Sender, Message, Receiver, Communication Barrier, Written Communication, Oral (or verbal) communication, Nonverbal communication, Symbol, Logical Appeal, Emotional Appeal, Ethical (personal) Appeal*, and more. I can envision biblical integration centered around these words and ideas.

11: Assessment and Biblical Integration

We have talked about syllabus design and unit planning, but how can we make sure that the biblical integration makes it into every lesson? The answer here is simple — assessment. In every course there are important tests, papers, quizzes, projects, or other graded assignments. If the syllabus lays out biblical integration goals, and if units are planned with integration in mind, then the course assignments must assess biblical integration.

Assessments do two important things for the teacher concerning biblical integration. First, they almost guarantee that the teacher will practice biblical integration. If the syllabus has established biblical integration as a goal and if the assessments will test the students' understanding of the integration, the teacher is motivated to integrate in every lesson. Second, assessing biblical integration allows teachers to see if they are truly being successful in biblical integration. If the assessments demonstrate understanding and growth, the teacher can be confident of success in integration. These assessments also show teachers areas to improve or adjust.

Look again at our adapted speech course description and try to identify areas of biblical integration that could be assessed:

> *Speech is a course designed to teach students effective Speech Communication. Since speech is a powerful gift that reflects God's glory (Gen 1:3), a potentially dangerous weapon (Jas 3:5-6), a means through which we know the Lord (Gen 2:16-17), and an avenue for praise (Psalm 19:14), students will study responsible and ethical communication. Since the Good News is a message that must be shared (Rom 10:14) with people who see it as foolishness (1 Cor 1:18), students will learn how to articulate*

> *through delivering different types of speeches*
> *such as persuasive (Acts 17:17), demonstration,*
> *informative (1 Cor 12), oratory speeches (Matt*
> *5), interviews (Luke 1:1-4) and how to debate in*
> *parliamentary procedure.*

The students might be expected to understand that 1) speech is a gift from God, 2) it is a powerful tool that can be used for good or evil, 3) God has spoken to us and directed us, 4) we can use our speech to please God, 5) God cares about our speech, 6) the gospel is communicated through speech, and 7) different kinds of speech can be used to advance God's kingdom. There are certainly even more ideas that could be drawn out for the students to grasp. And it should be clear that each of these seven areas that could be assessed are only starting points. For example, if 1) speech is a gift from God, He may desire that we utilize that gift in specific ways. So, what are some ways that God wants us to use our speech?

These types of questions are excellent for assessment. They are biblical and clear. They are practical and worldview-focused. They are challenging and directing.

The truth is simple—we assess what we deem as most important in our classes. If we prioritize biblical integration in our assessments, we will prioritize it in our courses. Carnegie Mellon University's Eberly Center, points out that learning objectives (how the student should think and what the student needs to know) should correspond with assessments (tasks that measure how they think and if they know) and instructional strategies (activities that help students think and know).[212] Alignment is key. If Christian schools say they prioritize biblical integration, but do not assess it, the alignment is off.

---

[212]Carnegie Mellon University, "Whys & Hows of Assessment: Alignment," accessed May 19, 2017, http://www.cmu.edu/teaching/assessment/basics/alignment.html.

Discussion Activity: Assessment Design

An ongoing project is one excellent way to engage in integration assessment.[213] Consider again our speech class. An example of an ongoing project would be to tie each type of speech throughout the year around the theme of sharing the Good News. For example:

Assignment 1: Prepare and give an informative speech about the Person and work of Christ.

Assignment 2: Perform an interview to discover someone's personal religious beliefs.

Assignment 3: Prepare and give a persuasive speech in response to the questions/struggles discovered in the interview.

Assignment 4: Deliver an oratory speech telling your personal faith story.

Assignment 5: Engage in a debate on key worldview issues.

Note that that this kind of integration can be planned from the outset of the year. If you integrate assignments/assessments, your course will be more easily integrated throughout.

---

[213]Donovan Graham, *Teaching Redemptively: Bringing Grace and Truth into Your Classroom* (Colorado Springs: Purposeful Design, 2009), 215.

If you were teaching this speech class, how might you create another sequence of assessments to be used throughout the year? These might be about God's communication to us through Scripture, the need for healthy communication (encouragement, pure speech, honesty, etc.), the importance of non-verbal communication and God's non-verbal communication to us through nature, the use of speech communication to build up the church, or other topics related to our course's central questions.

Training 3

The Instigating Teacher

Learn to stretch and strengthen students by revealing conflict between the Christian worldview and other ways of looking at life. You will discover how to invite them into the fray within the safety of the classroom so that they can struggle and apprehend the truth by recognizing and appropriating it for themselves. Learn to go beyond giving answers to helping students get them for themselves.

12: Healthy Conflict and the Teacher as Trainer

We are living in a constantly changing culture. Technology and media have made ideas more accessible. Advertising has made ideas more compelling. Materialism thrives. Individualism reigns. Every voice has been given a megaphone and many anti-Christian voices are speaking most convincingly. For example, a University of Kentucky study in 2017 conducted research that showed that up to 26% of Americans are atheists.[214] This is a drastic rise from the results of previous studies.

Like the wider culture, the church has not been immune to the effects of worldview conflict. Cultural engagement expert and public theologian Owen Strachan identifies the predominant worldview of young people as, "Narcissistic Optimistic Deism."[215] Even within the church, many are clearly embracing a view of life that is self-absorbed and self-satisfying.

These ideas are already in conflict with the Christian worldview. The battle of ideas is already raging. Teachers need to understand that students fight it now. It will not wait until they reach "the real world." As teachers, we want to invite non-Christian ideas into our classroom so that we can help the students wrestle with them while they have our support. We want the conflict to happen here where we have home-field advantage. We need to help our students learn to think critically now so that they will have that skill to use throughout life. Brooke Hempell, senior vice president of research for Barna Group, says,

> The call for the Church, and its teachers
> and thinkers, is to help Christians dissect

---

[214]Will M. Gervais and Maxine B. Najle, "How Many Atheists Are There?" January 23, 2017, accessed May 19, 2017, https://osf.io/preprints/psyarxiv/edzda.

[215]Owen Strachan, *The Colson Way: Loving Your Neighbor and Living with Faith in a Hostile World* (Nashville: Nelson, 2015), 120.

popular beliefs before allowing them to settle in their own ideology. . . . Informed thinking is essential to developing and maintaining a healthy biblical worldview and faith as well as being able to have productive dialogue with those who espouse other beliefs.[216]

Students must struggle with ideas before settling into them. They will be strengthened by working to think through real and important questions. Just like athletes train and lift in the weight room to prepare for a game or season, students can benefit from strenuous worldview exercise. They need to become strong so that they can succeed in the battles of ideas.

To be successful as a biblical integrator, the teacher cannot just give answers. Offering biblical solutions, instead of having the students wrestle for them, would be like a coach lifting the weights for his team. It might be easier in the moment, but it does not prepare them for life. The teacher's role is to know how to help the students grow stronger in a healthy way. The trainer keeps track of the weight being lifted. He adds weight and prescribes repetitions at the right time and in the right way. The healthy difficulty of exercise in the weight room builds strength for the contest. Righteous wrestling with ideas in the classroom should function in the same way. In the end, this work will result in strong students who are ready for the tough questions of the world.

Discussion Questions

---

[216]Jeff Myers, "Research by Barna and Summit: Postmodernism and Secularism Influence Today's Christians," May 16, 2017, accessed May 19, 2017, https://www.summit.org/resources/articles/research-barna-summit-postmodernism-secularism-influence-todays-christians/.

What dangers might result from isolating students from other ideas/worldviews rather than helping them to wrestle with them?

What is an example of how you have been able to train students to struggle well with other ideas? Was your experience positive? What could have made it even better?

Discussion Activity: Starting to Wrestle

What questions/assignments might help students struggle with the following facts in the setting of our speech class?

In a recent Barna survey of those who attend church at least once per month and consider their faith as very important to their life, it was observed that even practicing Christians are not worldview-thinking Christians.

- 20% strongly agree that "Meaning and purpose comes from working hard to earn as much as possible so you can make the most of life"[217] and,

- 19% strongly agree that "No one can know for certain what meaning and purpose there is to life"

[217] Ibid.

13: Essential Conflict Questions

Christian schooling expert Doug Blomberg makes the case that, "Schools should evidence that education is ultimately not about information, but transformation, about discipling rather than disciplines..."[218] Education is meant to mature students into young people who are critically thinking and accurately judging according to the Word of God. One of the most important avenues of helping students grow is worldview conflict. Craig Hazen, founder of Biola University's M.A. in Christian Apologetics, points out, "Doubts are everywhere. Almost all of us have them. And when not properly addressed, they can be spiritually disastrous."[219]

It is not helpful for Christian schools to encourage students to follow Christ without giving them the opportunity to see the superiority of the Christian worldview in every arena. We want to encourage students to have faith, but faith must be understood as "holding firmly to and acting on what you have good reason to think is true, in the face of difficulties."[220] Faith is not blind trust. It is not belief without foundation. We must help students apprehend the good reason behind the Christian faith. Then, we must help them hold to that good reason when challenges arise. How do we accomplish this? Often, conflict is the answer. Blomberg and Stronks point out,

> Too often, in Christian schools as well, we
> start with material that has been cleansed

---

[218]Doug Blomberg, *Wisdom and Curriculum: Christian Schooling after Postmodernity* (Sioux Center, IA: Dordt College Press, 2007), 178.

[219]Craig Hazen and Larry Barnett, "Young People Are Indeed Leaving the Church," *Biola Magazine*, Fall 2016, accessed May 20, 2017, http://magazine.biola.edu/article/16-fall/young-people-are-indeed-leaving-the-church/.

[220]David Marshall, "The Marriage of Faith and Reason," in *True Reason: Confronting the Irrationality of the New Atheism*, ed. Tom Gilson and Carson Weitnauer (Grand Rapids: Kregel, 2013), 139.

of its uncertainties and ambiguities, its connection with rich real-life contexts. We "clean up" life for pedagogical purposes -- perhaps too often, sterilize it. We think our task as teachers is to determine the logical structure of knowledge and then to transmit this to our students, rather than to take their hands and lead them as together we explore creation.[221]

Life is complex. We do students no favors by trying to simplify the world for them because then we are removing them from what life is really like. Again, we see the importance of key questions—essential questions. Jay McTighe and Grant Wiggins clarify what these look like,

These questions are not answerable with finality in a single lesson or a brief sentence—and that's the point. Their aim is to stimulate thought, to provoke inquiry, and to spark more questions, including thoughtful student questions, not just pat answers. They are provocative and generative. By tackling such questions, learners are engaged in *uncovering* the depth and richness of a topic that might otherwise be obscured by simply *covering* it.[222]

Students need their curiosity to be provoked. Their minds need to be stimulated. They need to be put in a position to engage the process by asking questions of their own. Think

[221]Stronks and Blomberg, "A Vision with a Task," 115.

[222]Jay McTighe and Grant Wiggins, "Chapter 1: What Makes a Question Essential?" accessed May 20, 2017, http://www.ascd.org/publications/books/109004/chapters/What-Makes-a-Question-Essential%A2.aspx.

of how this might work in a history class that is looking at World War II. Wouldn't this be an excellent time for the students to wrestle with questions around God's goodness and sovereignty? In Daniel 4, we can see the Bible teach that "the Most High is sovereign over all kingdoms on earth and gives them to anyone he wishes." In fact, this statement is repeated multiple times in that chapter. So, how do we deal with Hitler? How could a good God want to put Hitler in charge of a nation? Or does the fact that Hitler did gain power show that God is not as in control as the Bible teaches?

Now, as a Christian teacher, I am sure that your mind is working as you use your more developed experience, theology, and knowledge to answer these questions. However, that is not the point. The point is to encourage the students to wrestle. Giving them our answers deprives them of the process. They don't need a cleaned-up history class. They need a place to struggle and be strengthen through their own journey.

Discussion Activity: Step into the Shoes of the Student

Imagine that you are now a student in the speech class that we have been using as an example. You have been placed in a group, and received the following assignment:

- Read Daniel 3:1-18 and take special note of Shadrach. Meshach, and Abednego's impromptu speech in verses 16-18.

- As a group, put yourselves in the shoes of Shadrach. Meshach, and Abednego. Imagine that the king had just addressed you in anger (verses 13-15). Then create an impromptu speech like they did to answer the king. Tell him why you will not be bowing down to his idol. (Note: you cannot copy their speech directly.)

- After you have presented, we will have a discussion about the importance of impromptu speeches from 1 Peter 3:15-16.

14: Designing Conflict Questions and Strategies

In each course, there are many worldview questions that will be naturally central or recurring. They will connect to the material and they will arise throughout. This gives the students time to look at them in different contexts from a variety of angles. Developing these questions is, after the syllabus, the most crucial element in integration preparation.

Remember, we want to develop biblically integrated courses. We do not want a group of unrelated integrated lessons. Just like academic content develops and builds over the year or term, so does the biblical integration. Bradley McCoy provides an example. He has worked to develop integration in some of his science classes based on the identity of a Christian scientist. Scientists are often portrayed as arrogant or mad in popular culture, so he has designed questions that bring those preconceptions about character into conflict. Concerning arrogance, he might prompt,

> Often when scientists are portrayed in movies or other forms of popular culture, they are characterized as being arrogant. Why might scientists appear this way to the general public? Is arrogance in fact a common trait of scientists? If so, what makes scientists prone to this bad trait and what steps can we take to avoid arrogance?[223]

Here McCoy has chosen to focus on character development for integration. This theme is then connected to several character-related issues that scientists are known for. He then asks questions that encourage the students to wrestle with these ideas themselves. They must investigate why

---

[223]McCoy, "Developing a Program-Level Faith nitegration Curriculum," 347.

scientists are often not thought of as examples of Christian behavior. And they must chart a course so that they can truly live into their role as Christians who do science.

It is helpful for teachers to identify areas of conflict related to their course and organize conflict questions and sub-questions to guide integration for the whole year. We can take the questions that were designed to show the aim and foundation of our speech course (part of the syllabus design) and develop them further by adding sub-questions. These might look like:

Where did speech come from? Why did God give it? What is its purpose?
- Do we have a responsibility to use speech as God intended?
- Do we view speech as a gift? Are we thankful?

What dangers are associated with speech? Why must speech be ethical and responsible?
- Can speech be damaging to others? If so, how?
- Can speech be damaging to self? If so, how?

What role does speech play in relationship? How does God speak to us? Why did God entrust us with the spoken message of Good News?
- Do we listen to God speaking to us through the Bible?
- Are we able to articulate the Good News well to others?

There are three main questions here and each has two corresponding sub-questions. This is likely enough to provide a basis for excellent integration throughout an entire year. We might even be able to address many of these questions in each unit of the class from a little bit of a different angle.

Questions provide a skeleton which will support biblical integration. Once questions have been developed for a course, the teacher needs to have some ideas on how to use those questions well. We need to ask them in appropriately challenging ways. We want the students to have to engage deeply with each issue. Here are some strategic ideas:

We might expose our class to some non-Christian ideas and ask, "In what ways does this go against the Christian worldview?" The goal is for them to grow in the skill of identifying worldview conflict. Another option is to present an idea or argument and ask students to "listen for the cracks." [224] In other words, we want them to critically examine an argument to see if it holds water. We could also ask the students to identify where an idea would lead if it were allowed to be fully accepted. Or we can engage in more direct conflict by playing Devil's advocate. There are numerous options. It is up to the teacher to determine which strategies will work as a part of their course.

---

[224]Dan Egeler, "Raising Daniels in a Secular Babylon," *Christian School Comment* 48, no. 1 (2016/2017): n.p.

15: You Are the System

The teacher is the engine that makes biblical integration work. There is no other structure or curricular system that can replace example, passion and relationship that the teacher provides. When a teacher thinks biblically and shows care for the students, the effect is powerful. Apologist Lee Strobel calls this kind of connection "conversational apologetics" and describes it by saying, "It's a relationship. It's creating a safe place where people in a friendship can talk, over time, about the issues they have. The obstacles, intellectually; the sticking points, spiritually."[225] The pastoral role of the teacher cannot be overstated.

We must truly care for our students. We must love them more than our subject area. We must spend time with them. We must share with them. We must desire to serve them. We are more than their professional educators. We are brothers and sisters to those who know Christ. And we are missionaries to our students who are lost. We are mentors to those with open eyes. We are much more than just academic teachers and technicians. In a passionate plea for pastors to love well, John Piper asks,

> Is there professional praying? Professional trusting in God's promises? Professional weeping over souls? Professional musing on the depths of revelation? Professional rejoicing in truth? Professional praising God's name? Professional treasuring the riches of Christ? Professional walking by the Spirit? Professional exercise of spiritual gifts? Professional dealing with demons? Professional pleading with backsliders?

---

[225]Wade Bearden, "Show, Don't Prove: An Interview with *The Case for Christ*'s Lee Strobel," April 6, 2017, accessed May 20, 2017, https://christandpopculture.com/show-dont-prove-interview-case-christs-lee-strobel/.

Professional perseverance in a hard marriage? Professional playing with children? Professional courage in the face of persecution? Professional patience with everyone?[226]

Let us be men and women who pray and trust, weep and consider, praise and treasure, plead and persevere, play and show patience. Our students need us. They need biblical integration. And they need to see it consistently and compassionately displayed in us.

---

[226]John Piper, Brothers, *We Are Not Professionals: A Plea to Pastors for Radical Ministry* (Nashville: B & H, 2013), ix-x.

About the Author

Kelly Nathaniel Hayes

Kelly is a teacher and writer with experience working with all ages in school and church environments. He lives in Florence, SC with his wife, Jessica, and serves as the lead Bible teacher in the high school at The King's Academy. Passionate about worldview, discipleship, worship ministries, and artistic theology, Kelly has been educated at Liberty University and Seminary along with The Southern Baptist Theological Seminary.

Made in the USA
Monee, IL
07 May 2021